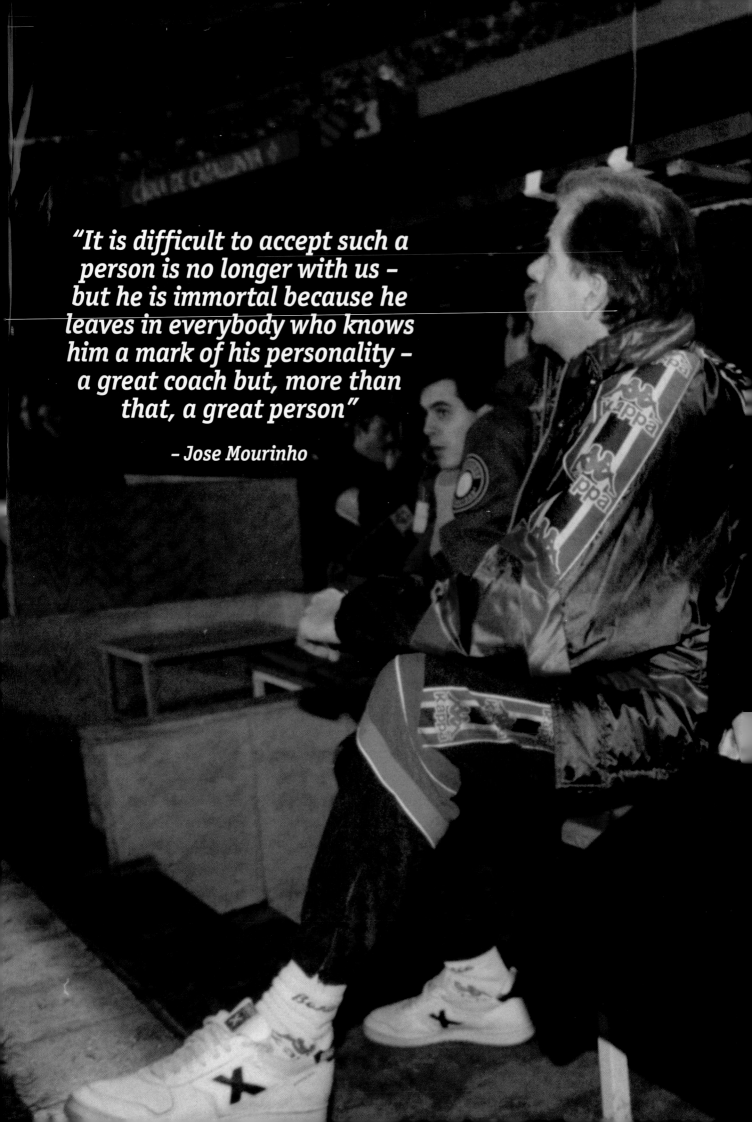

"It is difficult to accept such a person is no longer with us – but he is immortal because he leaves in everybody who knows him a mark of his personality – a great coach but, more than that, a great person"

– Jose Mourinho

A seventeen-year-old Bobby in May 1950, the summer before he made his Football League debut for Fulham

Savouring victory in Europe after
his Ipswich Town team had
beaten Dutch side AZ 67 Alkmaar
to win the UEFA Cup in 1981

*"I was never too big or proud to ask him for advice, which he gave freely and unconditionally. And I'm sure I am speaking for a lot of people when I say that. In my 23 years working in England there is not a person I would put an inch above Bobby Robson. I mourn the passing of a great friend; a wonderful individual; a tremendous football man and somebody with passion and knowledge of the game that was unsurpassed"*

*– Sir Alex Ferguson*

Nessun Dorma. A crying Gazza. An agonising penalty shoot-out before losing to West Germany. These are the memories of the Italia 90 World Cup when Bobby Robson was England coach at the height of his career. He united a nation. He gave the country a glorious sporting summer. And he came within a kick of reaching a World Cup final which most experts think England would have won. As a club manager he won the FA and UEFA Cups with Ipswich. Abroad, he twice won the Dutch and Portuguese leagues, the Spanish Cup and the European Cup Winners' Cup. But the tributes that have been paid were as much to Sir Bobby the man as to his talent as a manager. All those who spoke of him remembered his kindness, his generosity, his humour, his passion for football and his love of life. The Geordie gent, the son of a miner, will be sorely missed, and not only in Newcastle and Ipswich where he is still revered. He will be missed by the whole country.

# CONTENTS

A share of the profits from this special tribute publication will be donated to the Sir Bobby Robson Foundation, which raises money for the early detection and treatment of cancer .

A Mirror publication
**Marketing Manager:** Fergus McKenna
**Mirrorpix:** David Scripps and Alex Waters
020 7293 3858

Produced by Trinity Mirror Sport Media,
PO BOX 48, Liverpool L69 3EB
0151 227 2000

**Exectutive Editor:** Ken Rogers
**Senior Editor:** Steve Hanrahan
**Senior Art Editor:** Rick Cooke
**Senior Production Editor:** Paul Dove
**Compiled and written by:** William Hughes and James Cleary
**Designer:** Glen Hind

Part of the Mirror Collection
© Published by Trinity Mirror
**Images:** Mirrorpix, PA Photos
Printed by PCP

# A MAGNIFICENT OBSESSION

BY OLIVER HOLT

THE first time I went to Barcelona to see Bobby Robson after he had been appointed manager at the Nou Camp, he arranged for me to meet him at a training session at the stadium.

It was early in his only season in full charge at the club and he was still as full of the wide-eyed wonder of the place as any man new to its majesty would be.

He showed me around the dressing rooms and out on to the pitch where he spoke to the players in a hilarious kind of Spanglish that was a trademark of his time in Catalonia.

Then, because he was still getting to know the city and its environs, he asked his interpreter and assistant if he would drive us back to his home in Sitges, a few miles down the coast.

When we got there, he asked the interpreter to drive me to my hotel. I said I'd take a taxi but Mr Robson insisted. "Jose will be happy to do it," he said.

Jose Mourinho didn't look that happy actually, but he did it nonetheless. He knew he owed Robson a massive debt of gratitude.

If Robson had not taken Mourinho under his wing in Portugal and employed him in Barcelona to be his eyes and ears in the dressing room, the odds are that Mourinho would never have made it as a manager. He had no pedigree as a player or a coach but Robson introduced him to football's high society, and gave him enough prominence to get a coaching job back in Portugal.

But Mourinho is just one of many who owes much to the generosity, the humanity and the incredible, infectious enthusiasm for football and for life that made Robson such a loved and respected character in English sporting life.

A young generation of football managers, men like Sven-Goran Eriksson and Gerard Houllier, beat a path to his door when Robson was manager of Ipswich in the 1970s and asked to study his techniques.

Robson welcomed them, showed them hospitality and allowed them to take notes on his training sessions as he masterminded the club's gallant and stylish challenge for the league title.

What a team it was that Robson built there, with Arnold Muhren, Frans Thyssen and Terry Butcher. What a passion he brought to the English game. He was often mocked when he became national manager, but in the 1986 World Cup, England were only knocked out in the quarter-finals by Argentina because Diego Maradona cheated – then scored one of the best goals of all time.

Four years later, after surviving a sustained bout of lampooning from the press, he led England to the semi-finals at the 1990 World Cup in Italy, harnessing the genius of Paul Gascoigne and the deadly finishing of Gary Lineker.

It was a shoot-out against the Germans that robbed him that time, but England's journey in that World Cup rekindled love for the game in England after the hooligan-blighted decades of the '70s and '80s.

In that sense, the Premier League also has much to thank Robson for.

He was the father of much that is good about the obsession with football in this country.

Football was his own magnificent obsession and it was only later in his life when he was fully appreciated for that, when people came to love him because the game meant so much to him.

That love for the game shone through everything. Some mocked him when he was in charge of Newcastle because he was seen as a soft touch – but they regretted it.

How Newcastle could have done with a man of his integrity at the helm these past few years, somebody who loved the club like he did and who respected its fans and its history.

I always respected him. It was impossible for it to be any other way. In 1996, when I was a junior reporter with little background in football, I was given the job of ghosting Sir Bobby's column during the European Championship in England. He was never anything but incredibly kind, courteous and friendly to me and his columns were a doddle. His enthusiasm and knowledge of the game took care of that.

And when he got the Barcelona job, the crowning moment of his club career, he remained the same.

The second time I went to visit him there, I stayed at his house in Sitges with him and his wife Elsie, and listened spellbound to his stories of his life in football.

By then, he didn't need Mourinho to guide him around the city and one night, after an evening game at the Nou Camp, we drove back along the coast.

In some ways, it's my fondest memory of him, stopping at a toll at the entrance to a long tunnel on the coast road and seeing the face of the Barcelona supporter who took Sir Bobby's money.

As we drove off, he called after us. "Visca Barca, Go Barca," he yelled and his words carried on the night air. I looked at Sir Bobby, and he was grinning from ear to ear.

The last time I saw him was at Wimbledon last year. He was standing, a little unsteadily, with his son near the exit to the car park across the road from the All England Club.

His smile was as warm as ever and he asked after a friend of ours, another newspaper journalist, who had become his pal.

We chatted about football too and then he pointed at a man pushing an empty wheelchair, who was heading towards him.

"I'll have to say goodbye now, son," he said. "My Maserati's here."

12

# A TRUE HERO, ON AND OFF THE PITCH

BY SUE CARROLL

FOR a lot of Geordies, it will seem like losing their dad. For all England fans, a father figure.

Sir Bobby Robson will be mourned as the gentleman of football.

He'll be mourned by Elsie, his loving, always loyal and devoted wife of 54 years who was at his side right to the very end.

He'll be mourned by his three adored sons, Andrew, Paul and Mark, and their families.

Naturally, he'll be mourned by generations of football fans.

And he'll be mourned by me, forever grateful that he allowed my father's ashes to be scattered over the sacred turf at St James' Park.

Like my dad and so many strong Geordie men, Sir Bobby will be remembered for what he was. A brave and bonnie fighter right till the end.

No man could have clung onto life or loved it more than football's most devoted servant.

And even though he knew this, his fifth bout of cancer would be his last, he defied it, seeing the recurrence of this brutal disease as just another challenge in an existence littered with epic battles fought against all odds in the turbulent world of football – and mostly won.

His most recent, raising a staggering £1.2million for a cancer research centre at Newcastle's Freeman Hospital was fuelled by a determination to make this centre in his native North East not just the best in England, but the best in Europe.

His original target of £500,000 had been raised in just seven weeks.

Typically, he gave the money-raising project his all – he wouldn't have known any other way – but modestly attributed the achievement to the "goodness of the people", many of whom had simply put money into his hands as he and Elsie went about their everyday business.

"I have had fivers and tenners thrust at me in the street from people I've never met before," he recalled in wonder.

"Football makes a huge difference to people in this region, but football is about beating your opponent. This is about beating death."

It was a sign of this uncomplaining giant of a man that even at 76 he didn't realise the "goodness of the people'" was inspired by his own generous heart and the love felt for him across this region.

It was apt that when Sir Bobby did lose his fight he was surrounded by the people he loved, in the place he loved and was born, the Tyne Valley. It was here he would remind people that football "burrowed deeper into my body than any disease ever will".

He will be remembered, rightly, as a national hero. But it's us Geordies who will forever claim "Wor Bobby" as our own.

A local hero not just for his sensible, hands-on stewardship of Newcastle United, but because he epitomised everything good about North Easterners.

The indomitable spirit, the gritty determination to succeed and the ability to laugh in the face of adversity. All qualities reflected in every wise move Sir Bobby made and every word he spoke.

The son of a miner, Robert William Robson was born in Sacriston on February 18, 1933, and grew up in nearby Langley Park, a pit village on the outskirts of Durham City. His love affair with football started as a rite of passage many Toon lads will recognise. As soon as he was old enough, he made the 20-mile bus journey with his dad to St James' Park and he'd stand in line waiting for the gates to open at the Gallowgate End, clutching a ham sandwich and a mug of tea – come rain, hail, snow or blow.

This was the golden era of football when the game really deserved to be called "beautiful". A time when players were motivated by love of the game not money and, one suspects, Sir Bobby would have preferred it to stay that way.

This Saturday pilgrimage with his father Philip was more than a mere initiation into the Toon – it gave him that first taste of adrenaline which was to be his driving force.

He loved the poetry of football, the smell of liniment, the dedication of players and roaring approval of devoted fans whose passion and commitment he always valued, wherever his job took him.

Few men have lived, breathed and slept football as Sir Bobby did. More than half a century after those childhood trips to watch the likes of Milburn, Shackleton and Stubbins weave their magic, he took over at the helm of Newcastle United and pulled the club back from the brink.

He was 66, but the honour was tinged with just one regret – his dad never got to share it with him. "He had passed away when I got the Newcastle job. For him to see me manage the club he used to take us to watch would have been the thrill of his life. He loved the team. If he'd cut himself he'd have bled black and white." What, you can't help wondering, would the teetotal, non-smoking Philip, who missed only one shift in 51 years down the pit, have made of the game now, with its towering egos and millionaire players, some still teenagers? Like his son, he might have felt when money comes too easily, it can destroy.

Keeping players' feet firmly on the ground, and inspiring in them a passion for winning was always Sir Bobby's priority, claiming his role as manager involved being psychiatrist, psychologist, father, confessor, priest and occasionally dictator.

**Bobby the player:**
Pictured in Fulham strip, who he served with distinction in two spells spanning 11 years

14

**Top job:** Leading a training session with the England squad during the mid-1980s

15

"I strive," he once said, "to make them appreciate that, in my day, players fought against the maximum wage. I say to them: 'Go outside and see how hard it is to get a job at £10,000 a year, not £10,000 a week. Go to the job centre and see how hard it is'." Memorably, he once took his players down the replica coal mine at Beamish museum in County Durham so they could see where he came from. They didn't much like it.

Nor, in truth, did the young Bobby, who started his working life as an electrician at Langley Park colliery.

When 18 months later he was offered a career as professional footballer by Fulham, he admitted it wasn't so much an opportunity as an escape.

A goalscoring midfielder, he became a top player at Fulham, and later West Brom. He was canny too – the first player to negotiate an 'image rights deal', earning him a fee of three guineas for his photo to appear on cigarette cards. He won 20 England caps and played at the 1958 World Cup in Sweden, but it's what he achieved off the pitch as a manager that will always define him.

To say he became one of the most outstanding English managers of his generation is an understatement.

After a false start in charge of Fulham, a job that lasted just 10 months, in 1969 he took the helm at Ipswich Town, moulding an unfancied team into one of the best in the country – and Europe.

He led them to FA Cup glory in 1978, beating Arsenal in the final, and followed it in 1981 by winning the UEFA Cup.

The following year Robson could not resist the FA's call to become England boss.

He caused controversy – and a long-running dispute – with captain Kevin Keegan by promptly dropping him, a decision the player first heard about in the media.

At the Mexico World Cup in 1986, England were beaten by Argentina, and Maradona's infamous 'Hand of God' goal. Unimpressed, Robson said: "It wasn't the hand of God, it was the hand of a rascal."

Four years later, at the 1990 World Cup in Italy, Bobby gave English football its greatest moment since 1966. He had already announced he was quitting after the tournament, and expectations back home were low.

But inspired by Paul Gascoigne and the goals of Gary Lineker, England marched on to the semi-final before that heartbreaking defeat by West Germany on penalties.

Bobby moved on to PSV Eindhoven in Holland, winning the Dutch league twice, then on to Sporting Lisbon and Porto in Portugal, where he won yet more championships – it was at Lisbon that he first took a young interpreter called Jose Mourinho under his wing. In 1996 he took over at Barcelona, leading them to Cup Winners' Cup success in Europe.

And in 1999 he came home, in every sense of the word, taking over Newcastle at the age of 66.

When he arrived, the club was in danger of sliding out of the Premiership and sinking under the weight of a £44m debt. Within two-and-a-half years Bobby had reversed the nosedive. Those who doubted the wisdom of appointing an OAP were proved emphatically wrong, and in 2003 the club finished third in the top flight.

Now Sir Bobby – he was knighted in 2002 – when he became chairman Freddy Shepherd's scapegoat, ignominiously sacked in football's endless merry-go-round, the Robson-shaped hole left at the club has never been filled.

Meanwhile, he kept on working, taking a job alongside Republic of Ireland manager Steve Staunton.

"My wife wants me to go to Tesco's on Saturdays," he said in 2007, "but I just couldn't. I need the drug."

**Below:** Offering his advice to a group of Ipswich Town youngsters, 1982

He worked with many of the greatest players of the last two generations: Beattie, Butcher, Bryan Robson, Gascoigne, Lineker, Shearer, Romario, Ronaldo, Stoichkov, Figo, Van Nistelrooy, Guardiola and countless more. Maybe he didn't always remember their names (famously after calling Bryan Robson 'Bobby' the player replied: "No, I'm Bryan, you're Bobby") but his patriarchal interest in his team, though it sometimes meant dispensing old fashioned discipline, was legendary.

"Anyone who has played under him owes him a debt of gratitude," Alan Shearer said. "I certainly do."

As the great and the good line up to honour this remarkable man, I hope tribute is also paid to the woman Sir Bobby would have called the wind beneath his wings.

Lady Elsie was a nurse when they met at a Saturday night dance in Langley Park.

They married in June 1955. Every night of their lives Elsie, a Catholic, prayed for her husband. She had reason to. Bobby's mortal soul may never have needed the Good Lord's help but his body, over the years, has been desperately broken by cancer.

"I've spent my life trying to outwit the other team," he once said, "so I saw cancer as the opposition and I had to beat it." God knows he tried. The first bout came when, at 59, cancer of the colon was diagnosed. He didn't understand the implications of it. Or the unfairness. He never smoked. He didn't drink.

"It was the first time cancer had appeared in our family," he said. "None of my four brothers had it. My father lived till he was 86, my mother was 85.

"It didn't cost me a second thought. I just faced it, had it removed and moved on." Three years later, while working in Portugal, doctors discovered a malignant melanoma on his face.

"I didn't know what they were talking about — malignant melanoma sounded like a player for Benfica," Bobby said later.

If only.

It was August 1995 and doctors told him that unless they operated, he'd be dead by January.

Surgeons cut around his nostril, severed his lip, took his teeth out and removed the roof of his mouth.

He would need to wear a prosthetic device, a plastic frame called an obdurator, to keep his face in shape for the rest of his life. Without it, speech would be impossible and his face would collapse.

No one except Elsie would ever see his tears of frustration as he tried time and again to fix the painful device into his mouth.

But finally he cracked it — and to an unsuspecting world Bobby looked right as rain. Returning to work, surgeons told him, was not an option. Their words: 'Nobody ever works again after this operation, you're 62 so pack it in,' were like a red rag to a bull to a man nowhere near ready to plant vegetables in the garden.

Four years later, Bobby, still hungry for action, was back in the North East and at the helm of his beloved Newcastle United.

It wasn't until 2006 and during a skiing trip with his grandson Alexander that a bruised rib, suffered in a fall, revealed something far worse after a routine X-ray.

Doctors acted swiftly to remove a third of the right side of his lung after they found a tumour the size of a golf ball.

Even to Bobby, a man who had always appeared to treat cancer as a mild dose of flu, the signs were not good when a few months later a twitch in his face turned out to be the result of a brain tumour. In 2007, when he must have believed he'd kicked the disease into touch, Bobby was told a collection of small nodules on his lung were inoperable.

"How long have I got?" he asked. The answer was entirely dependent, doctors explained, on how they were able to control the tumours. But their best prognosis was 24 months.

"The doctors can't understand it," he said recently when asked about his extraordinary endurance and fortitude. "They think I'm a rare guy." The medics were spot-on. Knowing his time was limited, Bobby devoted his remarkable energy to raising cash for the fight against cancer.

Just five days before he died, he turned out at his beloved St James' Park for a charity match between England and Germany, featuring stars from his own Italia '90 side.

By now he had finally accepted that cancer was going to kill him.

"I have accepted what they have told me and I am determined to make the most of what time I have left," he stressed.

"I am going to die sooner rather than later.

"But then everyone has to go some time, and I have enjoyed every minute."

And so have we, Sir Bobby. So have we.

**What could have been:** Speaking to the media after Maradona ended England's World Cup dreams in 1986

# The Life of Bobby

**February 18, 1933**
Robert William Robson is born in Scariston, County Durham.

**May 1950**
Signs professional terms with Fulham. Newcastle United and Middlesbrough were also interested but, in Bobby's opinion: "Newcastle made no appreciable effort to secure my signature." He made his first-team debut against Sheffield Wednesday in November. Despite a pro contract, Bobby continued to work as an electrican.

**June 1955**
Marries Elsie.

**March 1956**
After scoring 68 goals in 152 games for Fulham, he transfers to West Bromwich Albion for £25,000 – then a club record transfer fee.

**November 1957**
Makes England debut against France, scoring twice in a 4-0 win.

**June 1958**
After finishing as the Baggies' top scorer with 24 goals in 1957/58, he starts three of England's games in the 1958 World Cup in Sweden.

**April 1961**
Scores England's first goal in the 9-3 demolition of Scotland in the British Home Championship. He scores again in an 8-0 defeat of Mexico a month later, his fourth and final goal for his country with his last cap, his 20th, coming against Switzerland in May 1962.

**August 1962**
Re-signs for Fulham for £20,000. His spell at West Brom saw him hit 56 goals in 239 appearances, also captaining the club for his last two seasons.

**1962 - 1967**
Scores 9 goals in 192 appearances in his second spell for Fulham.

**January 1968**
Becomes Fulham's manager after a brief spell with the Vancouver Royals in Canada. Bobby couldn't halt Fulham's slide into the Second Division though, and found out he had been sacked in November by reading 'Robson sacked' on a newspaper placard.

**January 1969**
Appointed Ipswich Town manager. Bobby guided the club to the Texaco Cup in 1973, the FA Cup in 1978 and the UEFA Cup in 1981. During his 13-year reign, he brought in only 14 players, preferring to help players develop through Ipswich's youth programmes.

**July 1982**
Succeeds Ron Greenwood as national manager two days after England were knocked out of the 1982 World Cup. Bobby was in charge of England for 95 games until 1990, winning 47, losing 18 and drawing 30 of those games.

**July 1990**
Leads England to the World Cup semi-finals, where they lose on penalties to West Germany. Awarded a CBE for services to football.

**1990 - 1992**
Moves to Holland to coach PSV Eindhoven, with the mission statement of bringing discipline to a fractious squad. PSV claimed the Dutch Championship in 1991 and 1992.

**July 1992 - December 1993**
Moves to Sporting Lisbon, guiding the club to third in his first season. A young Jose Mourinho acts as his Portuguese interpreter.

**1994 - 1996**
Having been axed by Sporting Lisbon despite the club being top of the league for the first time in 15 years, he is hired by FC Porto, with Mourinho appointed as his assistant manager. Porto went on to beat Sporting Lisbon in the Portuguese Cup final, with a Portuguese Super Cup and double league title success following suit.

**July 1996 - 1997**
Appointed manager of Barcelona, taking Mourinho with him once again. Barcelona bagged the Spanish Super Cup in, the Copa del Rey and the European Cup Winners' Cup under Bobby's stewardship. He is voted European Manager of the Year for 1996/97.

**1998 - 1999**
Rejoins PSV on a short-term deal, having been moved upstairs in a general manager role for the 1997/98 season at Barcelona. He guides Eindhoven to a third-place league finish and qualification for the Champions League.

**September 1999**
Takes over at Newcastle United, following Ruud Gullit's resignation. With the Magpies rock bottom, his first game in charge at St James' Park sees Newcastle put eight goals past Sheffield Wednesday without reply. They finish 11th that season.

**2000**
Freddy Shepherd, Newcastle chairman, refuses a request from the FA to permit Bobby to manage England part-time after Kevin Keegan steps down.

**2002**
Robson becomes Sir Bobby as he is knighted for services to football.

**2002**
A life-size statue of Sir Bobby is unveiled opposite the Cobbold Stand of Ipswich Town's Portman Road ground.

**2002 - 2004**
Newcastle finish fourth, third and fifth in the Premier League, twice ensuring places in the Champions League qualifiers. He is dismissed as Newcastle manager in August 2004.

**2005**
Made an Honorary Freeman of Newcastle, which Sir Bobby went on to describe as "the proudest moment of my life."

**December 2007**
Awarded the Lifetime Achievement Award at the BBC's Sports Personality of the Year show.

**March 2008**
Launches the Sir Bobby Robson Foundation which, by November, had already raised £1million, with funding allocated to provide equipment for cancer projects in the North East of England.

**July 2009**
Awarded the Emerald UEFA Order of Merit award, presented to Sir Bobby on 26 July before the Sir Bobby Robson Trophy match.

**Born leader:** Bobby at 14 holding the 'Waterhouses FC' ball alongside his fellow team-mates

# BOBBY – THE PLAYING DAYS

ALTHOUGH BOBBY FAILED TO WIN HONOURS WITH FULHAM AND WEST BROMWICH ALBION, HIS TALENTS WERE RECOGNISED BY HIS COUNTRY, WINNING 20 ENGLAND CAPS, APPEARING AT THE 1958 WORLD CUP AND SCORING FOUR GOALS. AS AN INSIDE-FORWARD OR IN MIDFIELD, ROBSON SCORED OVER A CENTURY OF GOALS IN HIS CAREER

Pictured in Fulham strip at a pre-season photocall. He enjoyed two spells with the club, from 1950-1956 and 1962-1967

**Baggies boy:** In action during a Black Country derby against Wolves in the late 1950s (left), and lining up with his West Brom team-mates ahead of the 1960/61 season. Sir Bobby is seated middle row, third from the left with his future coaching ally Don Howe standing back row, first right

PAGE 20   DAILY MIRROR, Monday, April 17, 1961

## Mirror SPORT — 4 PAGES

### England hope to keep hat-trick hero..

# ITALY MAY DELAY GREAVES DEAL FOR A YEAR

> "I played with him in the early 60s and he was a marvellous player. He was so in love with the game in every way and he will be missed by all those who love the game"
>
> – Sir Bobby Charlton

**By KEN JONES**

JIMMY GREAVES, hat-trick hero of England's shattering 9—3 victory over Scotland, is not likely to join Milan FC in the proposed £100,000 deal with Chelsea until AFTER the World Cup finals in Chile next year.

I learned yesterday there is growing opposition among Italian clubs to the lifting of the ban on foreign stars—and it may well prove strong enough to defeat this move at the Italian League clubs' meeting in Milan on Thursday.

There seems a good chance that the opposition group will get the date for lifting the ban pushed back to July 1, 1962 ... when the World Cup series will almost be over.

If the ban stays it will be a shattering blow to Greaves. But there will be deep sighs of relief at Lancaster Gate where the Football Association feel that at last England have a side that can confidently take on the world—and a side of which the goal-grabbing Greaves is a key member.

#### Very Difficult

After proving at Wembley that he was worth every penny of that six-figure transfer fee, Greaves told me:

"It's very difficult. This is a great England side. And I want to be in it. But I can't throw away the chance of earning the sort of money that I will never get in this country.

"I can only hope that if I move to Milan they will let me off to play for England."

But if England do lose Greaves, the World Cup spotlight will switch to Johnny Byrne—the Crystal Palace star who has rocketed from Fourth Division obscurity to the brink of international fame.

Byrne was chosen yesterday among the eight players who complete England's nineteen-strong tour party for the summer games against Austria, Portugal and Italy.

England team manager Walter Winterbottom said last night: "All the players have been chosen for their ability to step right into our tactical system. Byrne for Greaves, George Eastham for Johnny Haynes, Stan Anderson for Bobby Robson, and so on.

"Unless there are any last-minute changes through injuries or a possible Cup Final replay, we hope to keep the team that beat Scotland for the game against Mexico at Wembley on May 10."

The shattering defeat of the Scots was the pay-off to a season of international success based on the 4-2-4 line-up for which Winterbottom went overboard two years ago.

#### Scots 'Sleep'

The Scots blame French referee Marcel Lequesne for a free kick decision that allowed Bryan Douglas to score the goal that ended their brief come back early in the second half.

I blame the Scots who "slept" while Greaves slid a short pass to Douglas through a line of arguing defenders. And I feel it would still have made no difference to a result that was on the cards as soon as the Scots paraded their shaky defensive set-up right from the kick-off.

Their plan appeared to be man-for-man marking. Yet I seemed closer to the England forwards from my seat high in the stand than some of the Scottish defenders.

Skipper Johnny Haynes was tremen-

**JIMMY GREAVES . . . walking off after his Wembley hat-trick.**

dous. He revelled in the wide open spaces that Dave Mackay gave him once the tough Scottish Spur abandoned defence in a vain attempt to boost his attack.

Right from the start, Haynes struck up a perfect understanding with Greaves and centre forward Bobby Smith, who flitted into every gap to collect the shrewd, defence-splitting through-passes from his skipper.

And Greaves has never looked so deadly. Yet his best effort didn't produce a goal. It was a scorching shot that brought one of the few good saves out of Wembley's saddest man—Scots goalkeeper Frank Haffey.

Scorers: England.—Greaves 3, Smith 2, Haynes 2, Douglas, Robson. Scotland.—Mackay, Wilson, Quinn.

### The tour party

THE England party, announced yesterday for the summer tour games with Austria, Portugal and Italy, is:

**GOALKEEPERS**
SPRINGETT ................. Sheff. Wed.
HODGKINSON ............... Sheff. Utd.

**FULL BACKS**
ARMFIELD ................... Blackpool
McNEIL ..................... Middlesbrough
ANGUS ...................... Burnley

**HALF BACKS**
ROBSON ..................... W.B.A.
SWAN ....................... Sheff. Wed.
MILLER ..................... Burnley
FLOWERS .................... Wolves
ANDERSON ................... Sunderland

**FORWARDS**
DOUGLAS .................... Blackburn
CONNELLY ................... Burnley
GREAVES .................... Chelsea
EASTHAM .................... Arsenal
SMITH ...................... Tottenham
HITCHENS ................... Aston Villa
HAYNES ..................... Fulham
BYRNE ...................... Crystal Palace
CHARLTON ................... Manchester Utd

### HITCHENS COMES IN AT No. 9

GERRY HITCHENS (Aston Villa) at centre forward for Bobby Smith, who plays for Spurs in the Cup Final on the following day, is the only change in the English side for their match with Young England at Stamford Bridge on Friday, May 5. Teams:

ENGLAND: Springett (Sheffield Wed.), Armfield (Blackpool), McNeil (Middlesbrough), Robson (W.B.A.), Swan (Sheff. Wed.), Flowers (Wolves), Douglas (Blackburn), Greaves (Chelsea), Hitchens (A. Villa), Haynes (capt.) (Fulham), Charlton (Man. Utd.).

YOUNG ENGLAND: Macedo (Fulham), Angus (capt.) (Burnley), Ashurst (Sunderland), Shawcross (Man. City), McGrath (Newcastle), Moore (West Ham), Paine (Southampton), Hill (Bolton), Byrne (Crystal P.), Robson (Burnley), Harris (Burnley).

### FIXTURES

**FIRST DIVISION**
Tottenham v. Sheff. W. (6.5) .....

**SECOND DIVISION**
Sunderland v. S'thampton (7.15) ....

**THIRD DIVISION**
Halifax v. Q.P.R. (6.45) .....
Shrewsbury v. Newport (7.30) ....

**FOURTH DIVISION**
Barrow v. Gillingham (6.0) ....
Mansfield v. Doncaster (6.30) ....
Stockport v. North'pten (7.30) ....

### CROWD STOPS GAME

JOHN CHARLES (Juventus) and Eddie Firmani (Internazionale) played for only thirty-two minutes in a vital Italian First Division match at Turin yesterday.

Then a steel fence broke, the record 60,000 crowd overflowed to the pitch and the game was abandoned.

One man from each Italian First Division team will be tested for drugs tomorrow—after a "doping" complaint by a top official.

**Finest moment:** Bobby was amongst the goalscorers as England crushed Scotland 9-3 at Wembley in April 1961

**On England duty:** Sir Bobby shields the ball from Brazil star Mazola during the 0-0 draw at Ullevi Stadium, Gothenburg at the 1958 World Cup in Sweden

**Below:** Lining up with his team-mates ahead of the 1-1 draw against Wales at Ninian Park, Cardiff, October 1961. Back row, left to right: Jimmy Armfield, Bobby, Peter Swan, Ron Springett, Ron Flowers, Ray Wilson. Front row, left to right: John Connelly, Bryan Douglas, Ray Pointer, Johnny Haynes, Bobby Charlton

23

24

**Above:** Bobby closes in on
Liverpool's Ian St John
during the 2-2 draw between
the sides at Craven Cottage
in February 1967

**Above:** In action during the 2-1 victory over Manchester United in September 1964, while (right) Bobby lining up for a pre-season photocall at Craven Cottage in August 1965

**Above:** Attempting to evade the challenge of Graham Lovett during Fulham's 2-1 win over Bobby's former club West Bromwich Albion at Craven Cottage, April 1966.

**Left:** On the run, in his latter days in West London

**Learning the ropes:**
Chatting to Johnny Haynes
during his early days in
management at Fulham

# MOVING INTO MANAGEMENT

AFTER TAKING UP A SUGGESTION FROM THEN ENGLAND MANAGER WALTER WINTERBOTTOM TO ENROL ON A COACHING COURSE AT LILLESHALL, BOBBY MOVED INTO MANAGEMENT WITH FULHAM IN 1968. HE LATER LED IPSWICH TOWN TO DOMESTIC AND EUROPEAN SUCCESS

**Tractor Boy:** Lining up with the Ipswich Town team in July 1969, soon after taking over at Portman Road

**Opposite, top:** Assessing the fitness of defender Mick Mills ahead of Ipswich's FA Cup third-round tie against Manchester United in January 1970

**Town flyers:** Sharing a joke with David Johnson and Kevin Beattie during the summer of 1975

**Opposite, bottom:** Relaxing in Guadalajara with other English managers who had travelled to Mexico to watch the 1970 World Cup. Bobby is joined by, from left, Dave Sexton (Chelsea), Alan Ashman (West Brom), Bertie Mee (Arsenal) and Don Howe (Arsenal's assistant manager)

*"Sir Bobby's legacy will continue forever. If you take his achievements and put them on a modern-day scale, he effectively took Ipswich Town into the Champions League eight times during the 1970s"*

*– Mick Mills*

*"I went on to play over 500 games for Ipswich in a side that drew inspiration from its manager. I could not possibly get my head round how my career would have gone had it not been for Sir Bobby Robson. I owe him everything and I only hope I can be guided by the example he showed me"*

*– George Burley*

31

PAGE 2    DAILY MIRROR, Monday, May 8, 1978

# GLOOM AND

DESPAIR: Young Arsenal supporter David Lennon sits in a deserted Wembley after travelling all the way from Dublin.

DEJECTION: Arsenal's Pat Jennings yesterday

# Fans salute their heroes and loser

IT was Soccer's day of joy and despair. Of agony and ecstasy.

**ECSTASY** for jubilant Ipswich as they paraded the FA Cup before 50,000 delirious fans.

**AGONY** for losers Arsenal as they put on a

**By DOUGLAS BENCE**

brave face for faithful supporters who still turned out to cheer.

The cup of joy bubbled over for Ipswich's Wembley warriors when they drove through the town in an open-top bus.

Fans roared and whooped with delight as

skipper Mick triumphantly held the gleaming trophy captured in Saturday 1-0 victory.

The town was splashed with blue and white streamers as the cup hoop team made its to a civic reception.

Manager Bobby son said happily: "is my proudest mome

Not that the recep for Arsenal at Islington Town Hall lacked lighter moments.

## Dance

Centre-half W i l l Young staged an promptu tap dance a policeman's hat a boater and his trunch as a cane.

And cheering fans side chanted: "Yo Never Walk Alone."

But while the play managed to put on smile, they were hid a deep sense of dis pointment.

Arsenal chairn Denis Hill-Wood vow "We'll be back next y

"It takes a slumber giant a couple of years wake up."

## Thatcher ge caught offsi

TORY leader Marga Thatcher failed to s any points when in viewed on BBC ra after watching Wembley final.

She praised the p formance of Ipswi Trevor Whymark.

But although W mark's name appea on the programme, missed the match cause of injury.

## MIRROR COMMENT

# The Cup that cheers

THE fiftieth Cup Final will be remembered for many years to come. For the very best of reasons.

Not just because the country cousins —Ipswich—so stunningly outplayed the city slickers—Arsenal—against all the odds.

But also because the 100,000 good-natured fans who crammed into Wembley made this the Friendly Final—the way soccer used to be.

There was none of the vandalism and violence which has dragged English soccer into disrepute. The mindless minority stayed at home.

The Friendly Final began with the fans singing "Abide With Me" in a

way that football crowds have not sung for many years.

And when it ended, the referee went on a lap of honour—instead of running for cover from the angry fans, as so many have to do.

A few high-spirited drunks staggered into the arms of the law.

But as a police spokesman said after the match: "Just for a change it was all beer and no bother-boys."

It was English soccer at its best. The way football was before a few hooligans turned it into a blood sport.

Remember the days when football was just good, clean fun—and the England players led the world?

**Why can't it be like that ALL the time?**

Cup Final Special—Pages 26, 27 and Back Page

DAILY MIRROR, Monday, May 8, 1978    PAGE 3

# THE GLORY

DELIGHT: Ipswich fans give their team a hero's welcome.

Pictures: MIKE MALONEY

## Blacks in gun terror

By PAUL CONNEW

TWO black youths were gunned down in a race hate attack yesterday.

The terror shootings came as a group of eight West Indians were walking to a party in Wolverhampton.

Three white men in a car suddenly pulled up, shouted abuse — then fired off a series of shotgun blasts.

Two of the West Indians were peppered with pellets.

Then, for five minutes, the gunmen relentlessly chased the terrified blacks.

### Patrols

The attackers pulled up three times to open fire but no one else was hit.

The wounded youths were later named as Levi Harvey, 20, and Peter Jamieson, 19, of Blakenhall, Wolverhampton.

Levi had 19 pellet wounds in his back and one in his head. Peter had 13 pellet wounds in his back.

Last night, as immigrant leaders announced plans to set up vigilante patrols in the town, three men were helping police inquiries.

A police spokesman said they were expected to appear in court today accused of attempted murder.

## END OF THE MONSOON..

BRITAIN'S May monsoon is over, the weathermen promised yesterday.

According to the forecast, today will be warm and sunny, with only the occasional shower.

Parts of the South of England were still knee-deep in flood water yesterday after the freak storms when more rain fell in a week than is normal for the whole month.

**WEATHER WORLD**

TODAY: Mostly dry with sunny intervals. Max temp 17C (63F). TOMORROW: Similar.

LIGHTS: Derby 9.11; Plymouth 9.18; Birmingham 9.14; Bristol 9.15; London 9.3.

### HOME

| | Max. Temp. | | |
| --- | C. | F. | Weather |
| Blackpool | 19 | 66 | Rain |
| Brighton | 15 | 59 | Sunny |
| Cardiff | 9 | 48 | Drizzle |
| Clacton | 14 | 57 | Cloudy |
| Douglas | 14 | 57 | Rain |
| Exmouth | 16 | 61 | Cloudy |
| Hastings | 16 | 61 | Cloudy |
| Jersey | 13 | 55 | Sunny |
| London | 16 | 61 | Fair |
| Lowestoft | 11 | 52 | Sunny |
| Scarborough | 11 | 52 | Sunny |
| Shanklin | 15 | 59 | Cloudy |
| Torquay | 14 | 57 | Sunny |

### ABROAD

| | | | |
| --- | --- | --- | --- |
| Athens | 17 | 63 | Rain |
| Barcelona | 17 | 63 | Sunny |
| Belgrade | 17 | 63 | Fair |
| Biarritz | 12 | 54 | Rain |
| Geneva | 11 | 52 | Fair |
| Gibraltar | 19 | 66 | Fair |
| Innsbruck | 11 | 52 | Fair |
| Las Palmas | 19 | 66 | Fair |
| Lisbon | 18 | 64 | Fair |
| Majorca | 19 | 66 | Fair |
| Malaga | 23 | 73 | Sunny |
| Malta | 19 | 66 | Sunny |
| Paris | 13 | 55 | Cloudy |
| Rome | 16 | 61 | Rain |
| Vienna | 15 | 59 | Cloudy |

33

**Cup that cheers:** Bobby and his Ipswich Town club enjoy their shock FA Cup win over Arsenal in 1978. The Daily Mirror's report of the team's homecoming is reproduced on the previous two pages

**A job for life:** Making headlines in the Mirror (below) after being told he can stay at Ipswich forever following their FA Cup triumph

34

# WHAT A LIFE!

## Robson is told: You can stay for ever

### By HARRY MILLER

IPSWICH want to keep manager Bobby Robson at Portman Road for life.

Chairman Patrick Cobbold made that clear before the first celebration bottle of champagne had even been emptied.

The respect and regard Ipswich have for the man who has taken the F A Cup to East Anglia for the first time was crystalised by Cobbold when he told me:

"Bobby has seven years to go on his contract. If he wants to stay for life with us, he can. We will be delighted.

"We are happy with him if he is happy with us.

"There is only one job we would release Bobby for. That is the England one. We would have to. It is like a Royal command.

"We take the view that, if you've got a good manager, you keep him. There are not too many of them about."

Robson, a 44-year-old Geordie, has been in charge at Portman Road for nearly ten years. He is only the club's fifth manager since the war, and Cobbold says:

"When you change the manager, it also means you change the staff. With people like Cyril Lea backing Bobby, we also have a first-class staff."

### Marvellous

Robson said: "That's typical of the club . . . they are marvellous people to work for."

Ipswich's emphatic victory finally killed the theory that Robson was never going to be a winner.

He admitted late on Saturday night: "When John Wark hit a post for the second time. I looked to the heavens and said — Don't turn against us again.'"

Robson had pushed young David Geddis wide to counter the threat of Sammy Nelson attacking down Arsenal's left flank and that proved the winning tactic.

So Ipswich return to Europe and are ready to make a determined challenge for the First Division championship.

West Ham's England midfield ace Trevor Brooking could be a possible target in the summer months.

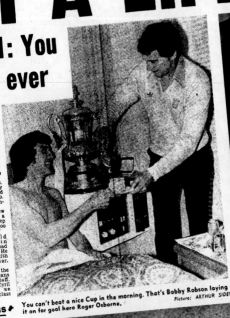

You can't beat a nice Cup in the morning. That's Bobby Robson laying it on for goal hero Roger Osborne. *Picture: ARTHUR SIDEY*

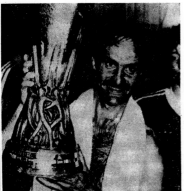

# IPSWICH NIGHT OF FRIGHT

## But they ride out storm and triumph

**From JACK STEGGLES in Amsterdam**

| A Z Alkmaar | 4 |
|---|---|
| *Welzl, Metgod, Tol, Jonker* | *Att: 28,500* |
| Ipswich | 2 |
| *Thijssen, Wark* | |
| H T : 3—2 | *Ipswich win 5—4 on aggregate* |

IPSWICH put themselves on the torture rack here in the Olympic Stadium last night as they were crowned UEFA Cup kings.

They made themselves — and their 7,000 travelling fans — suffer agonies before marching up proudly to collect the trophy.

It is a rich and fitting reward after a memorable season and Ipswich fully deserve the rapturous welcome home they will get today.

But for much of this second 'leg of a final that can only be described as bizarre they seemed to have a death wish.

We had been assured that the team with a reputation for wobbling when they had big leads in Europe would make no such mistake this time.

But it never worked out like that and some uncharacteristic defensive slips presented Alkmaar with gifts no team has a right to expect at this level.

Alkmaar — trailing by three goals from the first leg—had to throw every-

### Sweat

thing they had at Ipswich.

Ipswich had been warned to expect it. But they still did not seem prepared, and their faithful fans were in a sweat of anxiety on a hot steamy night with temperatures up in the 70s.

The Ipswich players were in a sweat as well, as Alkmaar put them under fearful pressure in a bid to save the game — which always seemed likely.

Their manager George Kessler had demanded they run until their drop-

ped. And he could not have got more out of them.

Their all-out attacking left them vulnerable at the back — and Ipswich took advantage to grab the goals that gave them the trophy.

They could not have asked for a better start. With Dutch international Frans Thijssen celebrating his return "home" by smashing them into the lead after just four minutes.

Thijssen is in dispute with Ipswich and threatens to take his immense talents elsewhere.

If he does decide to leave he could not have

given Ipswich a better-going-away present.

That goal left Alkmaar needing five to win and should have taken all the pressure off Ipswich.

But it didn't. They allowed Alkmaar to equalise three minutes later, Kurt Welzl heading through a centre from Johnny Metgod after Paul Cooper came for a long through ball, failed to get it and was left stranded.

### Record

Alkmaar went ahead on the night after 24 minutes, when Metgod was allowed to rise unchallenged at the far post to head through a centre from Jan Peters.

Ipswich, facing only two men at the back, looking like scoring every time they went forward. And John Wark equalised for them with an overhead kick in the 21st minute.

It was his 14th goal in

Europe, equalling the record set by Jose Altafini, of AC Milan, in 1963.

More defensive and uncertainly allowed Pier Tol to restore Alkmaar's lead six minutes before half-time.

And the game was really thrown wide open when Jos Jonker scored

Alkmaar's fourth with a blazing 20-yard free kick after 72 minutes.

Alkmaar smelt blood now and moved menacing in for the kill. But Ipswich dug deep into their reserves of courage to hold out and take the trophy.

Manager Bobby Robson acknowledged the

score they had had when he said: "We were on a knife edge.

"We needed the three goals we got in the first leg.

"They threw men at us from all over the place but they did not have any other option.

"I'm delighted for everyone at the club and

this goes a long way to make up for all the earlier disappointments we have suffered."

AT last they've got something to shout about . . . Paul Cooper (left), Frans Thijssen and Eric Gates forgot the disappointments of the last few weeks on Ipswich's glory night.

Pictures: MONTE FRESCO

Happiness is tinged with relief as Ipswich skipper Mick Mills lifts the UEFA trophy that Alkmaar tried so hard to snatch away.

**Opposite:** Shaking hands with Brian Clough ahead of the 1978 FA Charity Shield

**Euro joy:** Showing off the UEFA Cup to youngsters at Langley Park and, top, how the Mirror reported the game that saw Ipswich secure the trophy in the second leg in Alkmaar, May 1981

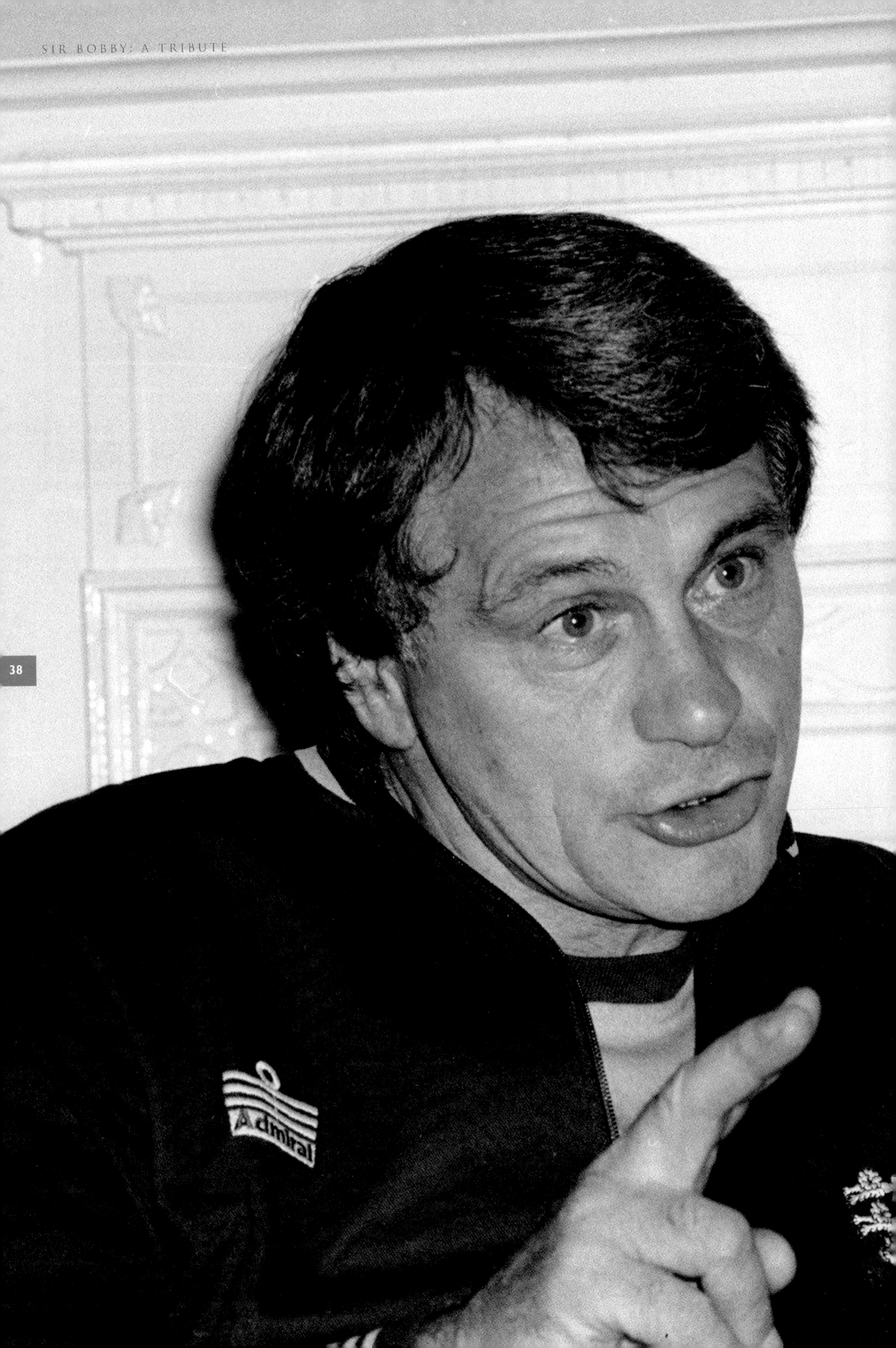
Admiral

# ENGLAND EXPECTS

NAMED ENGLAND MANAGER IN 1982, BOBBY EMBRACED THE JOB WITH TYPICAL PASSION. MARADONA'S MISCHIEF AND MAGIC SPELT DEFEAT IN THE WORLD CUP OF 1986, BUT FOUR YEARS LATER BOBBY'S ENGLAND TEAM WERE ONLY A FEW PENALTIES AWAY FROM REACHING THE FINAL

**Watching brief:**
Bobby sits alongside commentator Brian Moore in the TV studio to take in a 1984 European Championship qualifier between Hungary and Denmark

**Something brewing:** Joining Bryan Robson and Paul Mariner for tea in November 1982

**Bob's the job:** A young fan looks on in delight as Bobby obliges him with an autograph during a 1985 training session in Newcastle

**Making a point:** Trevor Francis listens in as Bobby offers advice on the training ground in September 1982

**Proud parents:** With mum Lillian and dad Philip before one of his final engagements as Ipswich manager at Middlesbrough in May 1982

**On top of the world:** Toasting qualification for the 1986 World Cup finals after beating Turkey 5-0 the previous day

42

**All smiles:** Enjoying a relaxing game of snooker in September 1985, and having a chuckle at a photograph of his Spitting Image puppet earlier the same year

# MIRROR SPORT

**1 a.m. SOCCER SPECIAL**

# GLORIOUS ENGLAND

## Lineker is the 3-goal ace

**From HARRY HARRIS in Monterrey**

**England 3 Poland 0**

MEXICO 86

LINEKER: Gave England a magnificent victory with a hat-trick.

**E**NGLAND last night rekindled the hopes of a nation when they qualified for the final stages of the World Cup.

And they gave a massive V-sign to the rest of the world who had written off our Mexican mission.

So from the wreckage of a disastrous defeat by Portugal, and a desperate draw with Morocco, manager Bobby Robson has re-built a team to give us back our pride.

And now they can go confidently forward to take on the other 15 super powers of soccer with their own belief gloriously re-born again.

### Scars

Old scars were re-opened with the embarrassing results from the opening matches with Portugal and Morocco.

So Bobby Robson decided to leave his team selection until the day of the match and, and, left out his ailing skipper Bryan Robson.

An unforgiving public had been demanding to know what had gone wrong on a mission that had left England with such hope and optimism.

And for the most important match England have played since 1982, Robson called for brave

hearts and stout resistance.

After five minutes the Poles showed their ability to break from defence, and Smolarek, the man Bobby Robson had feared forced Peter Shilton to save.

One minute later Poland carved out a clearer chance and once again it fell to Smolarek who with only Shilton to beat shot against the 'keeper.

But it was England who snatched a dramat-

ic eighth-minute goal in a marvellous breakaway attack.

Trevor Steven laid the ball out to Gary Stevens whose instant cross from the right was swept joyously into the net by Gary Lineker.

### Drive

And with the extra man pushing forward England could outnumber the static Polish side, who found the Everton pair of Stevens and Trevor Steven difficult to pin down.

When Peter Beardsley broke down the left in the 14th minute the Polish defence was torn apart and Lineker was able to sidefoot home England's second goal.

When the Poles won a free kick Smolarek took it, and drove in an effort that drew a sprawling save from Shilton.

But England were back at the throats of Poland, and Steve

Hodge had a goal disallowed after being set up by Stevens.

England could now afford to play with a confident belief in their ability, and their speed on the break, and the pace in which they cut Poland open, promised more goals.

Beardsley was a revelation for England, while Peter Reid supported him brilliantly to keep Poland under pressure.

Poland could not defend against such fluent football, and in the 35th minute England got a third goal.

Trevor Steven took a corner, the 'keeper fumbled and Lineker killed the ball on his thigh before burying it beyond Mlynarczyk.

Terry Fenwick was booked for a foul on Boniek, and now automatically misses England's next match as he dived in to make a typically abrasive challenge.

---

WIN £1,000,000

JVC VIDEO

## Scratch away at £1,000,000.

Buy a special twin pack of JVC E180 video tapes and you could end up a millionaire.

The twin pack contains a card. Just scratch the surface and you'll reveal the shirt number of a World Cup player.

You're then free to select the country you think most likely to reach the final with a player wearing that number.

And if your player makes the final and scores a hat trick, then you could be in the money.

There are also 100 other prizes of up to £1,000 worth of JVC products.

Plus 5,000 opportunities to win a unique Mexico World Cup souvenir.

With so much at stake it's well worth playing more cards.

So make your first goal your local JVC dealer. Then you can scratch away at your first million.

**JVC** MEXICO 86
Official Hi-Fi & Video Systems of the World Cup 1986
VHS

Published by Mirror Group Newspapers (1986) Ltd. (01-353 0246) and printed by British Newspaper Printing Corporation (London) Ltd., Holborn Circus, London EC1P 1DQ. Registered at the Post Office as a newspaper.     Serial No. 25,588    © The Daily Mirror Newspapers, Ltd., 1986

# MIRROR SPORT

MEXICO86

# CHEAT

**From HARRY HARRIS in Mexico City**

### England 1, Argentina 2

DIEGO MARADONA yesterday scored one of the great goals of the World Cup, but Mexico will always remember him for being a cheat.

The man they call the greatest footballer in the world handled Argentina into the semi-finals of the competition with a blatant act of cheating.

It was allowed by Tunisian referee Ali Bennaceur despite England's protests. Goalkeeper Peter Shilton indicated that Maradona had fisted the ball past him the instant the incident happened.

It was the goal that broke English hearts and three minutes later Maradona danced his way past three England defenders for a memorable second.

Yet there is no doubt that the incident in the 52nd minute changed the face of the match.

Maradona played a ball through the heart of the English penalty area, Steve Hodge tried to clear, but could only slice it back and Maradona accelerated forward. He clearly raised his fist to divert it over Shilton's challenge.

### Fist

Immediately he went on a lap of honour with his fist raised in triumph, while England's demoralised defenders vainly tried to draw the referee's attention to what happened.

Bobby Robson said: "We were so near yet so far. One was a dubious goal, the other a miracle.

"We couldn't get our game together, but give credit to Argentina. Yet I don't know how Gary Lineker missed that chance. If that had gone in, who knows what might have happened.

"We had to throw cau-

# Bandit Diego hands glory to Argentina

tion to the winds, but we lost to a very good team, and can hold our heads high."

England brought on John Barnes for Trevor Steven and a delightful piece of skill saw him send a brilliant cross over for Everton's Gary Lineker to head home in the 81st-minute.

But Lineker's sixth World Cup goal came just too late to save England from being

knocked out by the marvellous two-goal Maradona.

Lineker almost snatched a dramatic late equaliser from John Barnes's cross in a pulsating finish.

England went out complaining bitterly about Maradona's first goal, but the second, when he beat four defenders, destroyed Bobby Robson's team.

The Argentinian play-

ers went crazy with joy at beating England and avenging the 1966 quarter-final defeat.

Skipper Peter Shilton complained to the Tunisian referee that Maradona's 50th minute opening goal should not have counted.

But there could be no disputing Maradona's second and at the end the wonder-boy blew kisses to the crowd.

The little genius

ripped the heart out of an England defence that had conceded just one goal in the previous four World Cup ties.

Maradona tore past Peter Reid, Terry Butcher, Terry Fenwick and danced around Shilton for a goal that took Argentina through to the semi-finals.

But there can be no recriminations because England did their best. No England team has gone beyond the quarter-final stage in a World Cup abroad.

There had been so much disappointment in England's early performances that Bobby Robson's job was on the line.

The confidence of a team that were once the laughing stock of Mexico had risen after they had destroyed Poland.

And when Paraguay were beaten in the same way, a new and exciting belief swelled in English hearts.

Suddenly England believed they could live and compete with the best. And Robson's words of earnest enthusiasm that we were a match for any side in the competition had a clarion call of reality.

**OUT OF THIS WORLD—Pages 26, 27**

Published by Mirror Group Newspapers (1986) Ltd. (01-353 0246) and printed by British Newspaper Printing Corporation (London) Ltd., Holborn Circus, London EC1P 1DQ. Registered at the Post Office as a newspaper. Serial No. 25,597 © The Daily Mirror Newspapers, Ltd., 1986

# MIRROR SPORT

# CARRY ON ROBBO

**WORLD CUP SPECIAL**

## Sack him? Don't be daft says F.A. chief

**ENGLAND** manager Bobby Robson woke up yesterday fearing the sack.

Instead, he got the reward of an extended contract—probably through to the next World Cup in Italy, 1990.

Dick Wragg, chairman of the International Committee, confirmed the FA's 'Carry On' message to Robson.

Wragg said: "Sack him! Don't be daft. As far as I'm concerned, he's done a good job, and can stay on as long as he likes.

"It wasn't his fault we were robbed of a semi-final chance in Mexico. He'll see us through the European Champion-

**From HARRY HARRIS in Mexico City**

ship Finals in 1988 and probably the next World Cup, too."

Robson, who has a year to go on his present contract, had told the world yesterday: "I won't resign."

But he added: "Nothing shocks me. It wouldn't shock me if I wasn't asked to carry on. Whatever is decided. I will accept it. I am happy with what I have got.

"We have got to the last eight of the World Cup. Nobody should feel embarrassed or ashamed. We have been very close to a marvellous success.

"There is no doubt in my mind that I'm a better international manager now. I've learned how to cope.

"It is a very difficult job and I can understand why managers resign after the World Cup."

Robson stays behind in Mexico to watch the final stages of a tournament from which England won considerable credit after faltering badly early on.

---

*"To play for a manager like that – who was so loyal, and gave you so many opportunities – makes you feel hugely grateful and lucky. Privileged, really, to have played for one of the greats"*

**– Gary Lineker**

**A carry on:** The FA back Bobby after the 1986 World Cup, opposite page, and the England manager smiles for the cameras on arriving home after the tournament in Mexico

**Golden boy:** Presenting Gary Lineker with the golden boot after he finished as top scorer at the 1986 World Cup finals

47

**Robsons choice:** Bobby in conversation with his namesake and England captain Bryan in February 1987

48

**Cake that:** Receiving a 54th birthday gift from Gary Lineker and Bryan Robson in February 1987

**England managers:** With his good friend Micky Stewart, the England cricket manager, in 1987

**Cutting it:** In the recording studio with the England 1988 European Championship squad for the Stock, Aitken and Waterman-produced single All The Way. It peaked at number 64 in the charts

**Change the world:** Bobby is joined by Billy Bingham, Lawie McMenemy and Terry Venables for another 1988 musical venture

*"Having known him since the 1950s when he was transferred from Fulham to West Brom, where I was already, we just gelled together. He was a man of standards. Whatever he talked about or did, he had high standards to do the best he could possibly do and he lived his life that way"*

**– Don Howe**

**Chewing the fat:** Enjoying a chat with Dutch legend Johan Cruyff

**Howe's that:** Alongside his good friend Don Howe, who became a trusted member of Bobby's England coaching staff

51

# DAILY Mirror

Thursday, May 24, 1990    **COLOUR NEWSPAPER OF THE YEAR**    Average daily sale w/e: May 12: 3,914,261 (INCORPORATING THE DAILY RECORD)    22p

## Baby born to a 'dead' coma wife

**By FRANK CORLESS and JAN DISLEY**

A GRIEVING husband told last night how his "dead" wife was kept alive in a coma . . . until their daughter was born.

Mother-of-three Trisha Joseph, who was seven months pregnant, had been given no chance of surviving after a stroke.

Doctors kept her on a life-support machine for 33 hours until baby Holley was born by caesarian operation.

Then husband Theo, 39, gave the go-ahead for the lifeline to be switched off.

"Doctors told me my wife was brain-dead and asked me what I wanted to do about the baby," he said.

### Tragedy

"I knew of all the complications it could cause – but she had battled through her pregnancy. It's what she'd have wanted."

Theo, from Thornton, Blackpool, revealed that it was the second tragedy to hit the family in less than a year.

The couple's eldest son, 11-year-old Daniel, died from a brain tumour last autumn.

Trisha, 37 – a teacher at Blackpool's Montgomery School – was rushed to hospital with a haemorrhage on Friday.

Holley, who weighed just 3lb 3oz, is expected to stay in hospital until July.

# ROBSON IN 'I QUIT' SHOCK

## England soccer chief to join Dutch club after World Cup

QUITTING: England manager Bobby Robson

ENGLAND soccer manager Bobby Robson sensationally quit last night.

On the eve of the World Cup, he gave up the biggest job in football for a rumoured £250,000-a-year contract with a Dutch club – believed to be PSV Eindhoven.

Robson handed his written resignation to the Football Association yesterday – and it was accepted.

*The bombshell came just 24 hours*

**By DON MACKAY and PAUL SMITH**

before the England squad were due to fly to Italy.

A senior member of the FA admitted to the Mirror last night: "Robson is going.

"But he will still be in charge of our World Cup team.

"He will not leave until the week after the World Cup final is played.

"He is still determined to do his best for the England squad in Italy."

The senior official denied the England manager was leaving

for anything other than football reasons.

*Rumours were rife last night that Robson had quit because of an affair while he was manager of Ipswich.*

It was suggested that the soccer boss had offered his resignation because a woman, said to have been his lover, was now writing a book about the alleged affair.

But the official, high up in the FA, said: "The resignation has nothing to do with it.

"The only reason Bobby is leaving the England job is football."

Last night the 57-year-old father of three, who has been in charge of the international squad for the

● Turn to Page 2

**53**

**Time for a change:** Breaking the news of his May 1990 decision to resign as England manager once that summer's World Cup finals were over. Opposite is the Daily Mirror front page that appeared the following morning

*"He called me his Captain Marvel and it stuck for the rest of my playing career. It made me very proud but it was only typical of the respect he earned from myself and the rest of the dressing room. I have never come across anybody with such a passion for football. We had a tremendous personal relationship as manager and skipper. Any criticism he had of a player was kept very private and publicly he gave all of us his total backing. He will be missed by everybody who knew him."*

**– Bryan Robson**

**Tense times:** On the England bench during the 1990 World Cup semi-final against West Germany at the Stadio Delle Alpi

55

+WORLD CUP 90+WORLD CUP 90+WORLD CUP 90+WORLD CUP 90+WORLD CUP 90++WORLD CUP 90+WORLD CUP 90

# Great show, Gazza

● PAUL Gascoigne, the clown-prince of English soccer, is the most exciting new talent to have emerged in the World Cup finals.

● This message came from England boss Bobby Robson after his side's penalty shoot-out defeat by West Germany.

● Robson said: "Gascoigne has shown that he is one of the best players here.

● "He worked hard and learned. Had we got through he would have missed the final because of two bookings – and that would have been a tragedy for a very talented player."

# We would have
# WE HAD WORLD IN
# ENGLAND 1

## WEST GERMANY

**HERO**

ECSTASY for Gary Lineker after his brilliant equaliser. But the agony of defeat was to come.
Pic: ALBERT COOPER

**E**NGLAND had the world in their hands – and then saw it cruelly snatched away in an agonising penalty shoot-out here last night.

An historic place in the World Cup final was denied England as Stuart Pearce and then Chris Waddle missed penalties in a nail-biting semi-final showdown against West Germany.

England's World Cup campaign had ended in tears and heartbreak in the magnificent Stadio Dell Alpi in the cruellest way possible.

But the whole nation can be proud of this England team of heroes ... as they reached out for the summit of world football brimming full of guts, passion and commitment.

And Gary Lineker declared afterwards: "We can certainly go home with our heads high."

It was so near, yet so far for Bobby Robson's brave warriors as they came desperately close to taking their place in the final against Diego Maradona's Argentinian world champions.

England began the World Cup playing the sort of football that was condemned as stone age against the Republic of Ireland – but they finished it with a brand of sophistication that few believed they possessed.

### Proud

England not only matched, they, at times, outplayed the Germans – the best team in the tournament – and might have won.

For a manager who has been the most vilified in English football, Bobby Robson will be a proud man today.

Few expected England to reach the World Cup semi-finals and when they got there they graced the occasion.

The tears flowed as Pearce, in particular, seemed inconsolable.

Pearce hung his head in anguish and shame as his fierce penalty – England's fourth – struck goalkeeper Bodo Illgner

**From HARRY HARRIS in Turin**

on the legs, before, Olaf Thon converted and then Waddle blasted his kick over the top.

It was a sad, senseless way to go out but England are not alone in their suffering as the whole Italian nation has grieved since Tuesday when they lost in similar fashion to Argentina.

But that sadness must not mask how close England came to success.

England lost to Maradona's Hand of God goal four years ago in Mexico and this time by rights should be heading for Rome to avenge that in the 14th World Cup final.

Instead Robson's 95th and final match as England manager won't be the biggest occasion in world football.

It will be the consolation prize of the play-off for third place against Italy in Bari on Saturday.

# 'We can go home with our

+WORLD CUP 90+WORLD CUP 90+WORLD CUP 90+WORLD CUP 90+WORLD CUP 90++WORLD CUP 90+WORLD CUP

WORLD CUP 90+WORLD CUP 90+ WORLD CUP 90+WORLD CUP 90+WORLD CUP 90+WORLD CUP 90+WORLD CUP 90+WORLD CUP 90++

# crushed Argentina

# THE WHOLE OUR HANDS

## W. GERMANY 1

### WON 4-3 ON PENALTIES

## Cruel defeat for Bobby's braves

## Gary has a goal!

### By FRANK WIECHULA

● GARY LINEKER'S 80th-minute goal – his tenth in two World Cups – took him past some famous names like Brazilians Vava and Jairzinho, Paolo Rossi (Italy) and Eusebio (Portugal) in the all-time scorers list.

● The six-goal leading marksman in Mexico four years ago now stands joint fifth in the all-time World Cup rankings.

● The four players ahead of him are Kocsis (Hungary), Pele (Brazil), Juste Fontaine (France) and legendary West German striker Gerd Muller, who tops the list on 14 goals.

Robson will reflect with mixed feelings about this match and despite the defeat, it will fill him with deep satisfaction that his side almost beat West Germany.

Now Franz Beckenbauer will be aiming to become the first player and manager to win a World Cup, in the repeat final of four years ago.

West Germany have reached their third successive final, a record sixth final appearance, playing in a record 67th game in World Cup finals, surpassing Brazil.

England could not have taken on a more experienced country, or faced a tougher challenge in such an important match.

### Wobbled

With Mark Wright needing a special protective covering because of six stitches in a wound around his eye, Robson altered his defensive formation and started with skipper Terry Butcher as sweeper and Wright and Des Walker as the man-to-man markers.

Once again Wright

**SHILTON: Vital saves**

and Walker were superb at the back and Paul Gascoigne was marvellous in midfield, England's biggest success of the World Cup.

Gazza was reduced to tears by Brazilian referee Jose Ramiz Wright in the eighth minute of extra time when he was shown the yellow card for his foul on Thomas Berthold.

It meant that Gazza would have been ruled out of Sunday's final.

That proved academic, but at the time Gazza visibly wobbled, and was shaken so much that he could hardly play for the next few minutes.

England were also denied a penalty when Waddle was brought

down in the box by sweeper Klaus Augenthaler.

And it was Waddle who rattled the inside of the post in the 105th minute with a rasping left foot drive.

England rode their luck against Cameroon in the quarter final, but in Turin theirs ran out.

England had fallen behind to a fortunate opening goal, when Thon placed a short free kick to Andreas Brehme, whose shot took a wicked deflection off the foot of Paul Parker.

### Vital

Peter Shilton, a couple of yards off his line, got his hand to the ball as he fell backwards but couldn't stop it going in.

Shilton made two vital saves before Gary Lineker came to England's rescue once again.

With just ten minutes of normal time remaining and Steve Bull warming up, Parker's long searching pass embarrassed the West German defence.

First Juergen Kohler made an unconvincing

**END of a dream for England's Paul Parker and Stuart Pearce, who is consoled by coach Don Howe.**

contact and Augenthaler's challenge on Lineker failed as the Spurs striker took full advantage.

He sped past the German defence and fired a terrific left-foot shot into the corner.

In extra-time, Gazza regained his composure after his booking and he powered up the right flank only to be kicked up in the air by Brehme, who was booked.

Platt headed into the net from Waddle's free kick but was caught off-side.

Then as the game drifted towards penalties, with just three minutes to go Guido Buchwald curled a shot against Shilton's left hand post.

At the end of extra time, England's third successive two-hour stint in this tournament, Gazza collapsed to the floor knowing his World Cup was over no matter what happened.

The thousands of England fans in the stadium tried to lift his spirits by chanting 'We love you, Gazza'.

The Spurs star waved back to them but was in floods of tears and the England manager consoled him, deciding that he was in no fit state to be involved in the penalty shoot-out.

Lineker, Beardsley and Platt completed the nerve-wracking task of scoring from the penalty spot, but Brehme,

Matthaeus and Riedle converted theirs.

Pearce, a fierce striker of the ball, has a reputation of being deadly from the penalty spot, but his penalty failed and then Thon converted his.

The tension intensified for Waddle and his nerve broke as he fired over.

England had battled to the last – but in the end it just wasn't enough.

# heads held high°-Gary Lineker

+WORLD CUP 90+WORLD CUP 90+WORLD CUP 90+WORLD CUP 90+WORLD CUP 90+WORLD CUP

HARD LUCK LADS! + HARD LUCK LADS! + HARD LUCK LADS! + HARD LUCK LA

# MIRROR SPORT

# PROUD OF YOU

## Tears of despair

THE EMOTION shows on the face of the brilliant Paul Gascoigne, saluting the fans after England's cruel exit.
Picture: ALBERT COOPER

# England's cruel farewell

**E**NGLAND manager Bobby Robson emotionally admitted after England's cruel World Cup exit here last night:

"It's hard to keep the tears from falling. I am trying to hide them with a brave smile. I'm crying inside."

Robson had just watched his brave England side lose a dramatic penalty shoot-out 4-3 after the scores had been level at 1-1 at the end of extra time against West Germany.

## NIGEL CLARKE reports from Turin

England missed twice from the spot, and the Germans swept on to Sunday's final against holders Argentina. But England's glorious display left the whole country glowing with pride.

Added Robson: "It's nothing to be ashamed of. I'm just sorry that millions of people back home are crying with us too.

"There are tears and broken hearts in our dressing room."

Stuart Pearce was one of those weeping in despair and Chris Waddle was inconsolable.

Pearce saw his penalty somehow saved by West German goalkeeper Bodo Illgner while Waddle blasted his kick way over the crossbar.

Robson added: "It's a cruel situation. My heart goes out to Pearce and Waddle.

"But we graced a World Cup

◄ Turn to page 37

Published by Mirror Group Newspapers (1986) Ltd. at 33 Holborn, London EC1P 1DQ (071-353 0246) and printed by Mirror Colour Print Ltd. newspaper at the Post Office. **Serial No. 27,122** ©The Daily Mirror Newspapers, Ltd. 1990. Thursday, July 5, 1990. London Registered as a 0★

9 770956 805004

**National heroes:** The England squad ahead of the 1990 World Cup third-place play-off match against Italy. They are, back row, from left: Chris Waddle, Neil Webb, Mark Wright, Chris Woods, Peter Shilton, David Seaman, Dave Beasent, Trevor Steven, Gary Lineker, Steve Bull, Stuart Pearce, John Barnes, Terry Butcher, Bobby Robson (manager). Bottom: Des Walker, David Platt, Steve McMahon, Tony Dorigo, Paul Parker, Gary Stevens, Peter Beardsley, Paul Gascoigne and Steve Hodge

**Playing fair:** Showing off the FIFA Fair Play Award which England won at the 1990 World Cup finals

*"I'm devastated. Bobby was like my second dad. I was like a son to him. I can't describe how much he meant to me. He gave me a chance to play in the World Cup. I love him"*

*– Paul Gascoigne*

# ENGLISHMAN ABROAD

AFTER EIGHT YEARS AS NATIONAL TEAM MANAGER, BOBBY COULD RESIST THE LURE OF CLUB MANAGEMENT NO LONGER, ACCEPTING THE OFFER TO COACH PSV EINDHOVEN AFTER THE 1990 WORLD CUP. HE ENJOYED DOUBLE LEAGUE TITLE SUCCESS IN HOLLAND AND PORTUGAL WITH PORTO, BEFORE A LIVELY SEASON WITH BARCELONA

**Meet the boss:** Bobby signs autographs for fans in his early days in Eindhoven, July 1990.
(Opposite page) Under pressure at Barcelona before turning things around at the Nou Camp, January 1997

Mirror SPORT Mirror SPORT Mirror SPORT Mirror SPORT Mirror SPORT

# GET OUT

## Angry fans turn on Robbo

From TONY STENSON in Barcelona

**M**ORE than 70,000 screaming Barcelona fans last night turned on Bobby Robson – and could force him out of Spain and into the Newcastle job.

Robson suffered a torrent of abuse as Barcelona crashed to a 3-2 defeat against third-bottom Hercules. And watching Newcastle directors now feel Robson will change his mind and agree to take over from Kevin Keegan on a five-year £5million contract.

Fans cruelly stood and whistled protests at Robson, who earlier last night admitted that he was "having sleepless nights over the Newcastle job".

After this defeat he was locked in talks that could see him installed at St James's Park in the next 48 hours.

Robson told me before the match: "This Newcastle job is tailor-made for me."

He spent two hours with Barcelona chairman Jose Luis Nunez and will today give Newcastle his decision.

Last night he opened his heart to the Mirror, saying: "I've had so many sleepless nights recently. I do accept the Newcastle job is tailor-

← Turn to Page 35

**KEV**

**BY THE MAN WHO KNOWS HIM BEST**
**Page 34**

THE PRESSURE'S ON: Bobby Robson shows the strain during last night's shock Barca defeat in the Nou Camp

# COME IN

## But Geordies still want him

Published by MGN Ltd. at One Canada Square, Canary Wharf, London, E14 5AP (0171-293 3000) and printed by Mirror Colour Print Ltd. at Watford    Registered as a newspaper at the Post Office.    Serial No. 30,058    ©MGN, Ltd., 1995. Tuesday, January 14, 1997

61

03

9 770956 805523

**Cup of cheer:** Showing off the European Cup Winners' Cup alongside goalscorer Ronaldo following the 1-0 victory over Paris Saint-Germain in Rotterdam, May 1997

ROBSON salutes his match-winner Ronaldo

# Robson has a Euro joy night

**Barcelona 1
Paris St Germain 0**

BOBBY ROBSON leapt with delight after landing the European-Cup Winners' Cup in Rotterdam last night.

The former England manager, now 64, was then bear-hugged by his jubilant players.

Barcelona landed the trophy for a record fourth time and the streets of the Catalan capital were immediately the scene of celebrating fans. Among the chants was "Super Bobby."

Robson's future as Barcelona coach remains in doubt, but this was a triumph to savour.

"Barcelona are a club that must have success. We have given it to them so maybe some people will be pleased," Robson said in a thinly-veiled reference to demanding Barca President Josep Luis Nunez.

Had the victory saved his job? "That is a question you will have to ask the president. This helps. Not many presidents get given the European Cup-Winners' Cup every year," Robson said.

In fact, this was a record fourth triumph for Barcleona in the tournament.

Ronaldo, the world footballer of the year, scored the winner in the 37th minute.

The Brazilian's speed in the penalty box as he chased a pass from Luis Enrique first drew PSG defender Bruno N'Gotty into a blatant foul and the young striker then showed sufficient poise to get up to convert the spot-kick.

"I was just concentrating hard. I saw the keeper go one way and I put the ball the other," he said.

"It's my first title with Barcelona, so I want to enjoy the moment," he said.

Patrice Loko came closest to equalising for PSG with a shot against the far post.

## Pally is ko'd

GARY Pallister has been forced to pull out of Glenn Hoddle's England summer plans after learning he needs an exploratory knee operation.

The Manchester United central defender will undergo surgery on Friday amid fears he will again need a cartilage removed.

## Leav it out!

NEW Premier League chief executive Peter Leaver last night hit back at Middlesbrough chairman Steve Gibson after being accused of having "no idea" what football is about.

Leaver said: "I think I am right in saying Mr Gibson has never attended a club meeting."

# BACK WHERE IT ALL BEGAN

A PROUD GEORDIE, BOBBY HAS ALWAYS EXTOLLED THE VIRTUES OF THE NORTH EAST, SUPPORTING NUMEROUS WORTHWHILE CAUSES IN THE REGION THROUGHOUT THE YEARS. BOBBY ALSO SAW A LIFELONG DREAM FULFILLED WHEN HE WAS APPOINTED MANAGER OF HIS BOYHOOD CLUB, NEWCASTLE UNITED, IN 1999

**Greeting the people:** Bobby opens a new pitch extension at the Lightfoot Sports Stadium in Wharrier Street, Newcastle, March 1987

**Above:** Visiting a training centre for young people at Bearpark, County Durham, February 1987

**Back to school:** Bobby returned to his old village school in October 1982

67

Newcastle royalty:
Bobby with then
Newcastle United
manager Kevin
Keegan on the steps
of St James' Park,
December 1992

LEE: Gullit blast

# IT'S ROSY LEE, LOSING BOSS RUUD

**By JOHN WARDLE**

ROB LEE has admitted he was at an all-time low before Bobby Robson took over the reins on Tyneside yesterday.

He also joked about the bond he and Alan Shearer shared as they both felt the wrath of previous manager Ruud Gullit's time in charge.

The shunned Newcastle midfielder, who was not even given a squad number by Dutchman Gullit, was delighted to see former Robson appointed.

He said: "It will be a new beginning for me but then again things could not have been any worse, could they?

"I hope I'll get my chance now but we will have to see.

"I haven't had the opportunity to speak to Bobby yet but I am very happy he's here. But then again, I am always happy!"

Robson joined the

## SLOG ON THE TYNE
### Men in the St James hot seat

| | |
|---|---|
| JOE HARVEY | 1962-'75 |
| GORDON LEE | 1975-'77 |
| RICHARD DINNIS | 1977 |
| BILL McGARRY | 1977-'80 |
| ARTHUR COX | 1980-'84 |
| JACK CHARLTON | 1984-'85 |
| WILLIE McFAUL | 1985-'88 |
| JIM SMITH | 1988-'91 |
| OSSIE ARDILES | 1991-'92 |
| KEVIN KEEGAN | 1992-'97 |
| KENNY DALGLISH | 1997-'98 |
| RUUD GULLIT | 1998-'99 |
| BOBBY ROBSON | 1999- |

players at their Chester-le-Street training ground in County Durham after his announcement to the media yesterday.

And he vowed to give everyone a fair crack of the whip, including the former Charlton star who was brought in by Toon hero Kevin Keegan.

"I haven't spoken to Robbie individually yet but I will very soon," said Robson as he was chauffeured out of the training ground on his way to an FA dinner in London and on to Wembley today.

"I spoke to all of them today, not individually because there are too many there to speak to one-to-one.

"It will take time but I will do it."

Robson will also be speaking to Shearer, who was left on the bench by Gullit last week.

Lee agreed his pal would also be happy at the choice of manager, but said: "I have not spoken to Shearer yet."

He then joked: "In fact we don't speak that often – it is a myth."

# Robson: I thought was a big one but

**HANKY PANKY** Bobby Robson mimicking the gesture of fans in Spain who signal the end of a manager's job

# COME IN NO 9, AND WE'LL HAVE A CHAT

**By JOHN WARDLE**

BOBBY ROBSON will hold a private summit with Alan Shearer next week to reassure the England captain he is still Newcastle's number one strike weapon.

Shearer's relationship with Robson's predecessor Ruud Gullit deteriorated so badly that the £15million hit-man was axed for the momentous derby defeat by Sunderland last month.

And Gullit's walk-out on the Geordies seven days ago was due, in no small measure, to his power struggle with Shearer.

But Robson regards the Magpies skipper as a powerful ally, and the new Toon Army boss said last night: "When Alan comes back from England duty I will take the opportunity of talking to him about his situation at the club.

"He's had a lot of hysteria to

deal with and I need to reassure him that we still consider him to be a high quality international player.

"Everyone at Newcastle wants to see him get back on the goal trail and we've got to get him absolutely focused on that situation."

Shearer's ambitions to move into management were perceived as a major factor in undermining Gullit's authority.

And his adoption of an abrasive playing style led Tyneside legend Malcolm Macdonald to claim in The Mirror that Shearer was no longer fit to captain his country.

But Shearer had an excellent working relationship with Gullit's predecessors, Kenny Dalglish and Kevin Keegan, and club sources expect him to get on famously with Robson.

The former Ipswich and England boss rounded on Macdonald yesterday and, with echoes of Prince Edward's attack in America, said: "We are not a great country in terms of looking after our national heroes.

"In a week when England are playing two crucial games, and Alan is in the side as captain, I find it appalling that people are trying to knock him down. We should be right behind him."

IT'S GOOD TO TALK: Shearer and new boss Robson will meet early next week

THE MIRROR, Saturday, September 4, 1999    PAGE 91

# the Barcelona job this pips it for me

### Mike WALTERS

**M**ARBLES all present and correct, Bobby Robson was back on parade in English football's hard-hat area yesterday.

And as he skipped through Newcastle United's building site with a word-perfect performance, Robson struck a blow for Age Concern.

The old boy may qualify for a free bus pass, but there was no Zimmer frame in sight as Robson plunged back into English club management for the first time in 17 years.

He wants to stay "as long as my brain, my heart and legs work together simultaneously" but Robson looks as fit as a butcher's dog.

No wrinkles at 66 is a feather in any OAP's cap.

And, mercifully, there were no trips down Misery Lane to the days when 'Booby' Robson kept putting his foot in it as England manager.

Robson's only brush with ridicule this time was when he talked about the relative pressures of managing Newcastle and Barcelona.

Borrowing chief executive Freddie Fletcher's brown handkerchief, he waved it above his head and snorted: "When 110,000 people start doing this to you, that's what I call pressure."

Never mind that disaffected Catalans normally turn on their managers wielding exclusively white linen: for symbolism, Robson's gesture was as vacuous as Christian Gross pitching up at Tottenham by Tube and hailing his £3 investment on the Piccadilly Line as the "ticket to my dreams".

### Banana

Then there was an overwhelming temptation to compare Robson with Corporal Jones from TV's Dad's Army when he revealed that the keynote of his address to the players next week would be: "Don't panic — this situation is retrievable."

And at one stage he lurched into a runaway stream of metaphors which had begun with a sanguine observation about raising morale, confidence and team spirit.

Suddenly, imagery got the better of Robson as he spouted his determination to "plug a few holes, steady the ship, batten down the hatches, plug a few leaks and get the ship sailing again.

"I know what happens at football clubs, and particularly with players when the results don't come.

"You get on a banana slide and it's difficult to get off sometimes. The team desperately needs a victory.

HAPPY DAYS for Bobby Robson at Ipswich (above) with the UEFA Cup and with Bryan Robson and England (below) in the 1990 World Cup

WE'VE HAD KEEGAN DALGLISH AND GULLIT COME ON BOBBY WE CAN DO IT....

THE TOON Army were quick to give Robson their backing

## THE KING OF CLUBS
### Bobby Robson's managerial meanderings

**1933:** Born February 18, in Langley Park, County Durham.

**1950:** Joined Fulham. Made 152 appearances, scoring 68 goals. Moved on to West Bromwich, scoring 56 goals in 239 games.

**1958:** Played for England in World Cup in Sweden. Won 20 caps and one Under-23 cap.

**1962:** Rejoined Fulham, making 193 appearances (nine goals).

**1967:** Left Fulham in May to join Vancouver Whitecaps as manager.

**1968:** Took over as Fulham manager in January. Sacked in November.

**1969:** Appointed manager of Ipswich.

**1978:** Ipswich won FA Cup with 1-0 victory over Arsenal.

**1981:** Ipswich won UEFA Cup.

**1982:** Appointed England manager.

**1986:** England reached World Cup quarter-finals, losing to Argentina 2-1 thanks to Diego Maradona's 'hand of God' opening goal.

**1990:** FA revealed Robson's contract as England manager was unlikely to be renewed even if he won World Cup. Robson announced he would be taking over at PSV Eindhoven after tournament. England beaten on penalties in World Cup semi-finals by Germany.

**1991:** Won Dutch League.

**1992:** Won Dutch League before taking over as manager of Sporting Lisbon.

**1993:** Controversially sacked after a UEFA Cup defeat.

**1994:** Appointed manager of FC Porto, whom he takes to Portuguese Cup.

**1995:** Guided Porto to Portuguese League title.

**1996:** Steered Porto to second successive League title before resigning to take over at Barcelona.

**1997:** Presided over Barcelona's Cup Winners' Cup-winning campaign, but eventually surrendered coaching reins to Louis van Gaal and moved upstairs as Barcelona's general manager.

**1998:** Rejoined PSV as coach.

**1999:** February – offered to take over as England boss on a temporary basis after the sacking of Glenn Hoddle.

**September 1:** Spoke to Newcastle with a view to taking over from Ruud Gullit.

**September 3:** Confirmed as Newcastle manager.

TEAMING up with Ronaldo at Barcelona

---

"I thought Barcelona was quite a big job, but this has just pipped it." But just when you thought Robson's relish for the job he has coveted since boyhood was getting the better of him, and that an agile mind was giving way to senile twaddle, he reverted to common sense.

Sorting out Alan Shearer, whose relationship with Ruud Gullit became a squalid sideshow to Newcastle's wretched start, will be a priority.

Coping with the multilingual nature of Gullit's under-achieving squad will be another.

But it's nothing Wor Bobby hasn't seen before, and he said: "If the public see the players giving their best, I'm sure they will be patient and understand the situation. In the last nine years I've had five jobs abroad, and when I came home it wasn't my intention to retire, but to catch the ball if it came my way.

"When Kenny Dalglish was appointed here two-and-a-half years ago, I was sounded out, but it was the right job at the wrong time.

"For all I know, I might even have been in the reckoning a year ago, when Ruud Gullit was appointed, but I had just gone back to PSV Eindhoven a couple of months earlier. Who would have thought, a few years ago, that Kevin Keegan and I would swap jobs, with him taking on the England job and me coming to Newcastle?"

Ah, yes. Keegan. Said a few kind words about Robson 24 hours earlier, burying once and for all any lingering ill-feeling about their fall-out in 1982.

But peace in our time will have to wait until after the final whistle at Wembley today, when Robson will take up the VIP ticket reserved for ex-England managers as usual.

### Acclaim

Judging by the first day of the rest of his life, Robson will rekindle the feelgood factor which Dalglish stifled at Newcastle with his dire public relations, and which Gullit suffocated with his own ego.

Before he marched out to thunderous acclaim from Toon Army diehards, there was one last booby trap for him to negotiate.

Sitting next to chairman Freddy Shepherd, veteran of the Geordie Canine Defence League, Robson was asked by one pouting inquisitor what he thought of Geordie women.

Robson looked her up and down for a second, then replied: "Well, I'm looking at you, and I don't think you are too bad."

Only the sharpest charmers, and full sets of marbles, could have handled that one so adroitly.

## MAY-DAY SIGNAL
### FROM BACK PAGE

look at the players quickly, establish in my own mind what we need and instill confidence in them.

"We have a beauty of a match for our next game, at Chelsea, but we won't be afraid of it. The club hasn't enjoyed a victory for some time and needs one badly."

Surprisingly, 66-year-old Robson has been given a contract as team manager only until the end of the season, when he is likely to move upstairs as director of coaching.

He has not yet appointed an assistant, which leaves the door ajar for Peter Beardsley, Don Howe and Jose Maurinho, his No 2 at Porto.

But last night Newcastle's power-brokers were admitting he could turn out to be a short-term troubleshooter.

Chief executive Freddie Fletcher said: "There will be a complete review of all aspects of the playing side at Newcastle, and towards the end of the season Bobby's position will be discussed as part of that."

That could mean Newcastle looking for their fifth manager in three-and-a-half years next May.

---

## They said he was too old at 66, but the grey-haired Messiah has lifted the fog on the Tyne after just three matches

### Ian EDWARDS

**Newcastle 5 Sheff Wed 0**

BOBBY ROBSON has dreamed for 50 years of managing the club he loves but never could he have imagined a coronation like this.

After the adventures under Kevin Keegan, the dreary days of Kenny Dalglish, and the torment of Ruud Gullit's reign, the 66-year-old Messiah has transformed Newcastle in three matches.

The grey-haired pensioner has also achieved the seemingly impossible task of putting a smile back on the face of Alan Shearer.

Shearer must have wondered where his next goal was coming from during his in-fighting with Gullit.

He has cut a desolate figure, fighting against the critics who claim that, at 29, he is a spent force.

But the first five-goal haul of Shearer's career, which equals Andy Cole's Premiership record, transformed an emotional day into an unbelievable one.

Of course, it could cost Danny Wilson, another of

### PREMIERSHIP TABLE

| | P | W | D | L | F | A | Pts |
|---|---|---|---|---|---|---|---|
| Man Utd | 8 | 6 | 2 | 0 | 20 | 7 | 20 |
| Leeds | 8 | 5 | 1 | 2 | 14 | 9 | 16 |
| Arsenal | 8 | 5 | 1 | 2 | 11 | 7 | 16 |
| Aston Villa | 8 | 5 | 1 | 2 | 10 | 6 | 16 |
| Sunderland | 8 | 4 | 2 | 2 | 13 | 8 | 14 |
| Chelsea | 8 | 4 | 2 | 1 | 9 | 3 | 13 |
| Everton | 8 | 4 | 1 | 3 | 14 | 9 | 13 |
| West Ham | 8 | 4 | 1 | 1 | 9 | 4 | 13 |
| Tottenham | 7 | 4 | 1 | 2 | 13 | 10 | 13 |
| Middlesbro | 8 | 4 | 0 | 4 | 10 | 12 | 12 |
| Leicester | 7 | 3 | 2 | 3 | 11 | 10 | 11 |
| Liverpool | 7 | 3 | 1 | 3 | 10 | 9 | 10 |
| Southmp'tn | 7 | 3 | 0 | 4 | 10 | 13 | 9 |
| Watford | 8 | 3 | 0 | 5 | 5 | 8 | 9 |
| Derby | 8 | 2 | 2 | 4 | 7 | 14 | 8 |
| Wimbledon | 8 | 1 | 4 | 3 | 12 | 17 | 7 |
| Coventry | 8 | 1 | 2 | 5 | 10 | 13 | 5 |
| Bradford | 7 | 1 | 2 | 4 | 5 | 9 | 5 |
| Newcastle | 8 | 1 | 1 | 6 | 16 | 19 | 4 |
| Sheff Well | 8 | 0 | 1 | 7 | 3 | 23 | 1 |

football's nice guys, his job.

Shearer tormented woeful Wednesday with an 12-minute hat-trick in the first half to prove he is back to his lethal best.

And he rounded off the rout with the last two goals of Newcastle's biggest Premiership win, and their biggest win anywhere since the forties.

In just two weeks, Gullit's memory has been obliterated and Shearer's swagger restored by the tactical know-how of the man who used to stand on the terraces with his dad watching Jackie Milburn.

But even he could not have had any idea of the fantasy football that lay ahead as he took his bow on the pitch ten minutes before kick off.

Tanned and looking fit, the man who openly admitted to being envious at the men who have preceded him in the St James' Park hot-seat had the Toon Army eating out of his hands.

"Walking in a Robson wonderland," boomed all round the packed stadium as

Wednesday were torn to shreds in a basement battle that turned into a slaughter.

This was Newcastle's first league win since April 3, but although Shearer refused to feel sorry for Wednesday, Robson's consoling arm around the shoulders of Wilson on the final whistle told its own story.

Wilson's record of one point from eight matches, is almost certain to lead his sacking after 15 months in charge.

Wednesday's promising start and a strangely subdued Newcastle gave little hint of the carnage that lay in store.

But once Aaron Hughes headed his first goal on 11 minutes, Wednesday just collapsed.

The 19-year-old was left unmarked to convert the effervescent Kieron Dyer's cross from close range.

The loss of striker Andy Booth, stretchered off with his face covered in blood, after a collision with Alain Goma, did little to help Wilson's cause.

Within 15 minutes of his departure, their was no Wednesday cause left. It had been obliterated by Shearer who, for once, was provided with the service on which he

thrives. The England captain had managed one goal from the penalty spot against Southampton and his others had been against the civil servants of Luxembourg.

If he needed a confidence-boost, Wednesday's dejected defence was the perfect opposition.

All his predatory instincts were back when he flicked Nolberto Solano's low cross past Kevin Pressman with the outside of his right boot.

He added his second with a penalty after Emerson Thome was harshly adjudged to have handled Warren Barton's cross. And he com-

pleted his first Newcastle hat-trick for over two years on 42 minutes, pouncing in the six-yard box to force home another Dyer cross.

Shearer played a major part in the fifth goal too, before Dyer scored from close range.

Speed headed in Solano's corner for number six. Pressman gifted Shearer his fourth with a poor punch, and Steven Haslam's foul on Paul Robinson presented him with his fifth, a penalty.

**UNDER THREAT:** Danny Wilson

---

## How Shearer re-wrote the Premiership records

ALAN SHEARER yesterday became the second player to score five goals in a match since the formation of the Premier League in 1992, when Newcastle beat Sheffield Wednesday 8-0. The first to achieve the feat was Andy Cole who struck five in a 9-0 defeat of Ipswich in 1994-95.

**Other major individual scoring records:**

**10 GOALS IN A GAME:** Joe Payne for Luton v Bristol Rovers 1936 (Div 3 Sth)

**9 IN A GAME:** Robert 'Bunny' Bell for Tranmere v Oldham (Div 3 Nth)

**7 IN A GAME:** Ted Drake for Arsenal at Aston Villa 1935 (Div 1); James Ross for Preston v Stoke 1888 (Div 2); Tim Coleman for Stoke v Lincoln 1957 (Div 2); Tommy Briggs for Blackburn v Bristol Rovers 1955 (Div 2)

**6 IN A GAME:** Bert Lister for Oldham v Southport 1962 (Div 4)

**5 IN A GAME** includes: Barrie Thomas for

Scunthorpe v Luton 1965 (Div 3); Keith East for Swindon v Mansfield 1965 (Div 3); Steve Earle for Fulham v Halifax 1969 (Div 3); Alf Wood for Shrewsbury v Blackburn 1971 (Div 3); Tony Caldwell for Bolton v Walsall 1983 (Div 3); Andy Jones for Port Vale v Newport 1987 (Div 3); Paul Barnes for Burnley v Stockport 1996-97; Robert Taylor for Gillingham at Burnley (1998-99); Tony Naylor for Crewe v Colchester 1992-93 (Div 3); Steve Butler for Cambridge v Exeter 1993-94 (Div3); Guiliano Grazioli for Peterborough at Barnet 1998-99; Andy Cole for Man Utd v Ipswich 1994-95 (Premier).

**NEWCASTLE:** Harper 6, Barton 6, Domi 7 (Glass 83, 6), Goma 6, Hughes 6, Solano 6, Speed 6, Lee 6, Shearer 8, Ketsbaia 6 (McClen 78) Dyer 7 (Robinson 63, 6).

**WEDNESDAY:** Pressman 5, Newsome 5, Nolan 5, Walker 5, Thome 5, Sonner 6, Rudi 5 (Haslam 46, 5), Donnelly 5 (Siben 84, 5), De Bilde 6, Booth 5 (Carbone 27, 5), Alexandersson 5.

---

**RUUD GULLIT:** Reign over

## ENGLAND CANNOT DROP ME

FROM BACK PAGE

since the manager came in and everyone is playing with a smile on their faces," added Shearer.

Under-fire Wilson vowed to fight on after yesterday's horror show, but admitted: "I'm a realist and I don't know how many defeats like that we can take.

"That was the most humiliating defeat I have ever experienced in my career. I don't think it was a slaughter but it was certainly a bad day at the office.

"It's difficult to say to the fans 'stick with us' but I'm not at rock bottom. This just makes me more determined.

"I will hopefully be given the chance to turn the situation around and I intend to stick in there. But the question of my future is not one I can answer and this result won't help the chairman."

Wednesday's walloping was their heaviest defeat since they lost 8-0 at Middlesbrough 25 years ago.

Robson was more concerned about Wilson's future than his own side's astonishing revival.

He said: "I feel sorry for Danny Wilson and I hope the supporters and the club get around him. I hope they stick with him and let him do a difficult job."

## HODD WAITS FOR THE CALL

### By HARRY HARRIS

GLENN HODDLE is ready to take the Sheffield Wednesday job if it is offered to him.

Hoddle is the hot favourite to take over from under-fire Danny Wilson at Hillsborough, seven months after being sacked as England coach.

Hoddle has always said that he would need plenty of time to overcome the trauma of being fired by the FA. For months he was not interested in a return to the game, despite being linked with number of jobs.

But I understand that Hoddle is now ready for a fresh challenge and his credentials make him a perfect candidate.

His record as a club coach is impressive. After winning promotion as player-boss at Swindon, he became the catalyst for the current Chelsea revival.

Wilson's position at Wednesday has clearly reached breaking point after yesterday's 8-0 humiliation at Newcastle and his departure will leave the door open for Hoddle.

Leicester boss Martin O'Neill is also in the frame. O'Neill pledged himself to Leicester just days ago, although it is clear that he will move in the summer.

**Big impact:** Having been appointed Newcastle United manager in September 1999 following the resignation of Ruud Gullit, Bobby Robson's first home game in charge saw the Magpies crush Sheffield Wednesday 8-0 – the club's biggest victory since the 1940s. He was in the role for nearly five years, enjoying three top-five finishes having taken over with the club rock bottom of the Premier League

*"Sir Bobby Robson was a great man. I worked with him for five years every day. He was certainly the best manager I ever worked with at Newcastle. He never put me under pressure and always tried to see my side. He wouldn't put up with fools and didn't take any nonsense. He came across as a very kind guy but underneath was very tough. He thought about football 24 hours a day and would ring me at all hours of the day and never stopped thinking about football"*

**- Freddy Shepherd**

*"Bobby was a people's man. He could get on with anybody no matter what age they were and that says a lot about the kind of man he was, and why he was so highly thought of. He was held in high regard across the world not only for what he did in football, but for what he did in life. He was a winner, a battler and a fighter and he fought until the very last. I've got a lot to thank him for. He saved my Newcastle career – there's no doubt about that – and I'm just pleased I had the chance to tell him that and thank him for it"*

**- Alan Shearer**

**PM Visit:** With Tony Blair and Newcastle United defender Warren Barton at St James' Park, November 2000

**New Year 2002:** Bobby starts the fireworks from the Gateshead Millennium Bridge with local council leaders Mick Henry (left) and Tony Flynn

74

**Meeting of minds:** Sir Bobby
in conversation with Pele at
Northumbria University
Gallery, October 2003

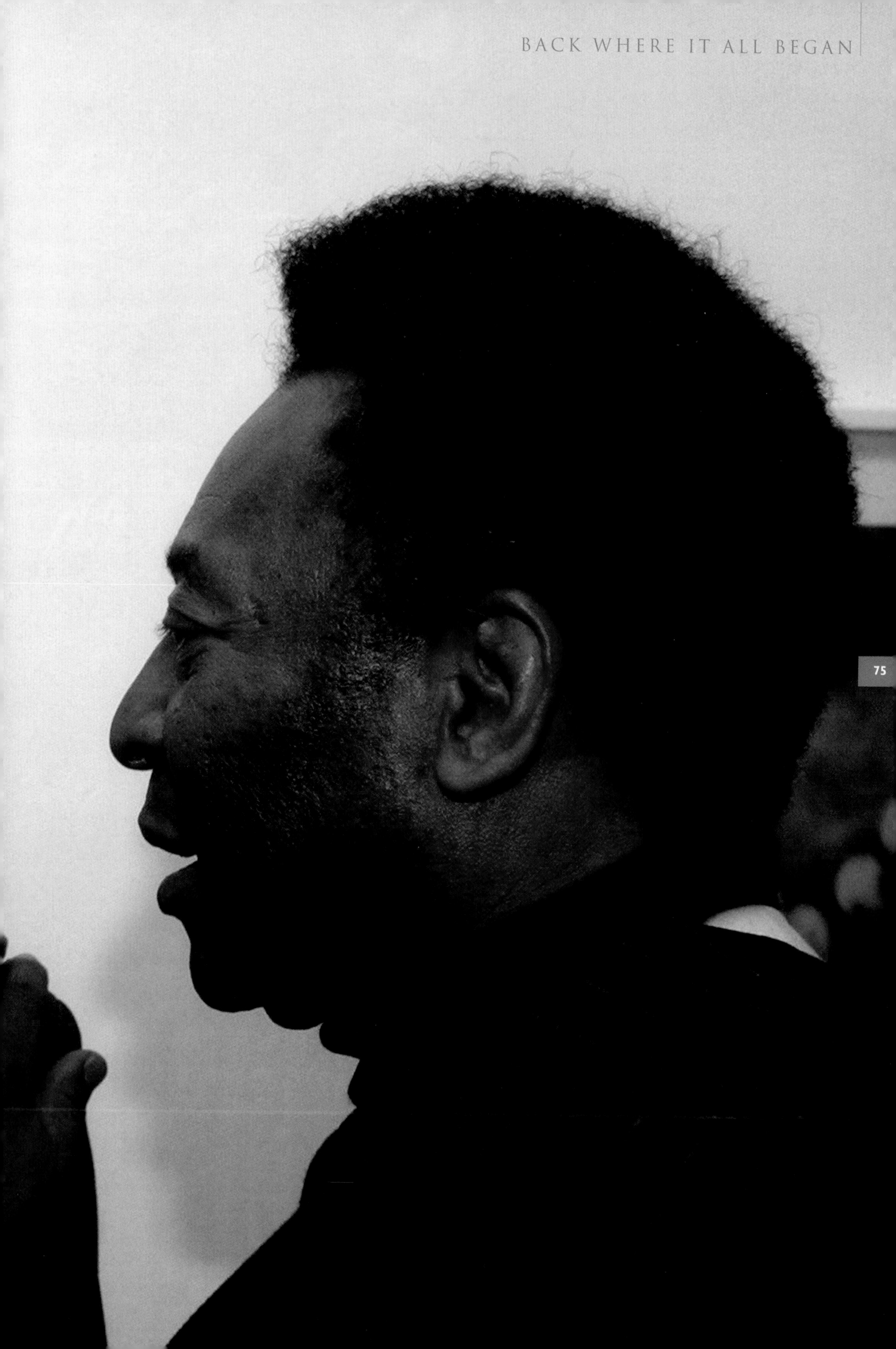

**Great greeting:** Sir Bobby started the 2007 Great North Run – as they passed, hundreds of runners reached up to shake his hand

77

**Above:** The Sir Bobby Robson Foundation was launched in March 2008, the aim of which is to aid the early detection and treatment of cancer, as well as trialing new drugs to help beat the disease. Over £1.6m has been raised so far

## COURT

▲ **LEADER** O'Neil Denton

# 9-boy gang caged for teen rape

**By ADRIAN SHAW**

NINE schoolboys were yesterday locked up for the horrific rape of a 14-year-old girl.

The thugs were as young as 13 when they took it in turns to assault their victim and record it on a mobile.

Gang chief O'Neil Denton, now 16, ordered the girl to be attacked last April as punishment for insulting his girlfriend, Snaresbrook crown court heard.

In an impact statement, the victim told how she has attempted suicide and lives in constant fear.

Rapists Denton, Weiled Ibrahim, 17, Jayden Ryan, Yusuf Raymond, Jack Bartle, all 16, Alexander Vanderpuije and Cleon Brown, both 15, and a 14 and 16-year-old who cannot be named, are all from East London.

Their sentences ranged from 29 months to indeterminate terms.

Judge Wendy Joseph QC said the rape was "designed to degrade and humiliate".

## IVF

▲ **MOTHER** Rajo Devi

# Baby at 70 for world's oldest mum

**By MARTIN FRICKER**

AN Indian woman aged 70 has become the world's oldest mother after giving birth to a baby girl.

Rajo Devi had her first child at the National Fertility Centre in Haryana in the north of the country.

Anurag Bishnoi, the doctor who supervised the IVF treatment which enabled her to conceive, told The Times of India that both the mother and child were in good health.

Rajo and her husband Bala Ram, 72, were delighted at finally having a family. "We longed for a child all these years and now we are very happy to have one in the twilight years of our life," said Bala.

Brushing off concerns about their age, he said: "We have a joint family as is common in rural Haryana." The couple, who married in 1954, said the "social stigma" of being childless had been lifted after the birth of their daughter on November 28.

# SIR BOBBY'S A HERO ..ONE OF OUR OWN

▲ **PROUD DAY** Sir Bobby with wife Lady Elsie and Durham mayor Grenville Holland yesterday

**INSPIRATIONAL** England manager Sir Bobby in 1988

## Brave footie legend honoured

BY **JEREMY ARMSTRONG**
jeremy.armstrong@mirror.co.uk

HIS full head of silver hair has gone and his face is lined by the strain of battling cancer for a fifth time.

But Sir Bobby Robson's warm smile lit up the room yesterday as he was made an honorary freeman of Durham.

Sir Bobby, 75, captured the heart of his home city by showing the same fighting spirit which made him a football legend.

He got a standing ovation at the town hall as mayor Grenville Holland told him: "You are one of our own. We are proud to have you in our midst." Describing him as "a local hero", Mr Holland added: "Nobody is more deserving of the freedom of Durham."

Sir Bobby, with wife Lady Elsie by his side, was honoured for services to football and

charity. He has raised more than £1million since he was diagnosed with inoperable lung cancer in 2007. He vowed to find treatments and set up a foundation in his name.

He was first diagnosed with cancer 16 years ago. On being told he had the disease for a fifth time, he said: "It's not the greatest news I've had but I'll battle as I've always done."

Sir Bobby began his football career while still at school in Langley Park, Durham. He signed for Fulham in 1950 and went on to play for West Brom and England. As a manager, he won the FA Cup with Ipswich Town before taking England to the 1990 World Cup semis.

He was made a Freeman of Newcastle three years ago and granted the Freedom of Ipswich last year.

▶ SIR Bobby's cancer foundation is funding a centre on Tyneside. To donate visit www.sirbobbyrobsonfoundation.co.uk.

**Voice of the Mirror: Page 10**

78

★

Daily Mirror
FRIDAY 20.02.2009 **SPORT** M 63

# SIR BOBBY ROBSON — FINAL CAMPAIGN

# THIS WILL BE MY PROUDEST LEGACY

## Stricken legend: £1.2M cancer centre eclipses anything I've achieved in game

▲ **SAVING LIVES**
Freeman Hospital in Newcastle, where Sir Bobby's cancer centre will open

▲ **SO BRAVE**
Sir Bobby has suffered from cancer five times

BY **SIMON BIRD**
simon.bird@mirror.co.uk

**SIR BOBBY ROBSON cracks a joke that when his doctor started to talk about malignant melanoma he thought it "sounded like the right-back from Benfica".**

Black humour was just one way of dealing with his five bouts of cancer, the latest of which has left him fighting on with inoperable tumours in his lungs. In the past 10 remarkable months, Robson has unleashed all his charm, persuasiveness, and love of life to help future generations beat the disease.

Today Robson will unveil a legacy that could eclipse even his wonderful 50 years of achievement in football.

Facing his own terrible personal journey, he made a difference to others.

The Sir Bobby Robson Cancer Trials Research Centre will be opened by the man himself at Newcastle's Freeman Hospital, alongside current England boss Fabio Capello. It proves football, with personalities like Robson, and all those donors who have chipped in, can be a powerful force.

Robson, 76, said: "We have a saying up here in the North-East: 'Shy bairns get nowt!'

"I am proud that this could be my legacy. The cancer has shown me the best of people.

"This disease can strike down any age – little children, teenagers, anyone. I have had my life, a wonderful life, but I want to help others get diagnosed quicker and treated better.

"There may not be a cure until well after I have gone but this will help. I am desperately proud that it is a facility in Newcastle, my city, my father's city, the city where football burrowed deeper into my body than any disease could."

Robson set up a website last March to kick off the fundraising and a steady stream of donations have flowed in since – many with moving dedications to lost relatives, friends and colleagues. It was a typically wholehearted response to a tentative request from his oncologist Professor Ruth Plummer, for help raising money for a new NHS cancer centre.

Robson is full of touching tales of people handing him notes in the street, and a collection by a wife at her husband's funeral that she personally delivered in an envelope to his house.

Robson has never missed an appointment or meeting during his difficult last few years. He has faced the operations and treatment with a football mentality. "Bring on the next match, the next opposition..." he says.

Robson has lived the last couple of years to the full. His doctors call him the "miracle man" because of his resilience. He's

> I am desperately proud that it is a facility in Newcastle, my city, my father's city, the city where football burrowed deeper into my body than any disease could.
>
> **SIR BOBBY ROBSON**

regularly watched football from the directors' box at Newcastle and Sunderland.

Will-power and inner-strength have kept him going. He used to wear a hat in public to hide the loss of his thick mane of grey hair, but not now.

Eight month ago Robson

was unsure whether he could even reach the £500,000 needed to kit out the centre, but the total was reached in just seven weeks and has now been doubled and more.

It will be bolstered further today when Capello presents a £75,000 cheque from the Football Association, with a glowing tribute.

Capello said last night: "Sir Bobby is a very courageous man. He is a football legend not just in England but around the world.

"I have known him for many years, from when we both managed in Spain, and I am very pleased that The FA are backing The Sir Bobby Robson Foundation.

"It is an honour to be able to present him with a donation which will help his Foundation's important work."

It is an honour that tens of thousands have felt privileged to share. Robson said last

night: "This is a particularly proud day for everyone involved. I don't just mean myself, my wife Lady Elsie and the charity committee and centre staff.

"Every single person who has made a donation to the Foundation, sponsored a friend or workmate or organised a fundraising event should be very proud too.

"This new Centre is our first major achievement together and it will make a huge difference to the experts who are working hard to find new treatments for cancer.

"We don't want to rest on our laurels. This is a wonderful new facility but the patients who come through its doors are at the very frontline in the fight against cancer.

"The best way we can continue to help them is to keep pulling together as a team."
**www.sirbobbyrobson-foundation.co.uk**

**SPORTS WIRE**
Bringing you updated reports & results from around the world

### Snooker

## Fu brings the Rocket down

RONNIE O'SULLIVAN crashed out of the Welsh Open yesterday – throwing away a 3-1 lead to Marco Fu.

The Rocket was in control at the Newport Leisure Centre until Fu rattled off four frames in a row to win 5-3 and book his slot in the quarter-finals.

Scot Stephen Maguire also won through.

### Rugby Union

## Boozy Henson in Wales frame

WALES are ready to forgive Gavin Henson ahead of his Six Nations return against France.

Henson, Andy Powell, Jonathan Thomas and Rhys Thomas were all reprimanded for drunken behaviour in Cardiff.

But Wales team manager Alan Phillips insisted: "It will not affect selection for the game."

### Golf

## Tiger's ready to roar back

WORLD No.1 Tiger Woods will make his long-awaited comeback from injury in next week's Accenture World Matchplay in Tucson, Arizona.

Woods, 33, has been out of competitive action since winning the US Open last June.

The following week he had reconstructive surgery on the anterior cruciate ligament in his left knee.

### Drugs in sport

## Ohuruogu: I'm right on tests

SPRINTER Christine Ohuruogu claims protests at new drug-test rules in other sports where competitors must state where they are for an hour each day "vindicates her".

Ohuruogu, who won 400m gold at Beijing after overturning a ban for missing out of competition tests, said: "I kind of feel vindicated as people are saying it's difficult."

### Cycling

## Cavendish is on the pace

BRITAIN'S Mark Cavendish sprinted to victory in stage four of the Tour of California.

Cavendish covered the 185.7km (115mile) stage in a provisional time of 4hr 43min 10sec.

Levi Leipheimer of the US keeps the overall lead.

---

## The life & amazing times of Sir Bobby Robson

▲ **LEGEND** Sir Bobby leads out West Brom, wins the FA Cup as Ipswich boss and goes on to manage Barcelona and England

▲ **HONOUR** He receives a knighthood in 2002

### His record in football

**AS A MANAGER: IPSWICH TOWN** FA Cup (1978), UEFA Cup (1981)
**PSV Eindhoven** Dutch title (1991, 1992)
**FC PORTO:** Portuguese Cup (1994) Portuguese title (1995, 1996)
**FC BARCELONA:** Copa Del Rey (1997) European Cup Winners' Cup (1997)
**AS A PLAYER:** Won 20 England caps, scoring four goals. Played for Fulham (1950-56 and 1962-66) and West Bromwich (1956-62)
Knighted 2002 for services to football

**Suits you, Sir:**
A proud Sir Bobby
Robson after receiving
his knighthood from
Prince Charles at
Buckingham Palace in
November 2002

# A NATIONAL TREASURE

SIR BOBBY'S CONTRIBUTION TO THE GAME WAS RIGHTLY RECOGNISED BY MANY - FROM HIS HOME CITY TO QUEEN AND COUNTRY. OUR TRIBUTE CONCLUDES WITH A ROUND-UP OF HIS ACHIEVEMENTS AND HIS PERSONAL ROLL OF HONOUR

**Local hero:** Sir Bobby receives the Freedom of Newcastle at a ceremony at the city's Civic Centre in March 2005

# SIR BOBBY ROBSON - A ROLL OF HONOUR

### AS A PLAYER:

20 FULL ENGLAND CAPS, FOUR GOALS
FOR FULHAM: 370 APPEARANCES, 80 GOALS
FOR WEST BROM: 257 APPEARANCES, 61 GOALS

### AS A MANAGER:

### WITH IPSWICH TOWN:

TEXACO TROPHY 1973, FA CUP 1978, UEFA CUP 1981

### WITH ENGLAND:

ROUS CUP 1986, 1988, 1989
WORLD CUP SEMI-FINALIST 1990

### WITH PSV EINDHOVEN:

DUTCH CHAMPIONSHIP 1991, 1992

### WITH FC PORTO:

PORTUGUESE CHAMPIONSHIP 1995, 1996
PORTUGUESE CUP 1994
PORTUGUESE SUPER CUP 1994

### WITH BARCELONA:

EUROPEAN CUP WINNERS' CUP 1997
SPANISH CUP 1997
SPANISH SUPER CUP 1997

### AWARDS AND HONOURS:

1990 – MADE A CBE FOR HIS SERVICES TO FOOTBALL
1992 - FOOTBALL WRITERS' ASSOCIATION TRIBUTE AWARD FOR AN
OUTSTANDING CONTRIBUTION TO THE NATIONAL GAME
2001 - BRITISH SPORTS WRITERS' ASSOCIATION PAT BESFORD TROPHY
FOR OUTSTANDING ACHIEVEMENT
2002 – KNIGHTED AND BECOMES SIR BOBBY ROBSON FOR HIS SERVICES TO FOOTBALL
2002 – AWARDED THE FREEDOM OF NEWCASTLE UPON TYNE
2002 – RECEIVES THE UEFA PRESIDENT'S AWARD FOR SERVICES TO FOOTBALL
2003 - INDUCTED INTO THE ENGLISH FOOTBALL HALL OF FAME
2005 – IS MADE AN HONORARY FREEMAN OF NEWCASTLE
2005 - LIFETIME ACHIEVEMENT AWARD FROM THE SPORTS COACH UK AWARDS
2006 - EIRCOM INTERNATIONAL PERSONALITY OF THE YEAR
2007 - BBC SPORTS PERSONALITY OF THE YEAR LIFETIME ACHIEVEMENT AWARD
2008 – AWARDED THE FREEDOM OF IPSWICH
2008 – AWARDED THE FREEDOM OF THE CITY OF DURHAM
2009 – RECEIVES UEFA'S EMERALD UEFA ORDER OF MERIT AWARD

Sir Bobby was the man the nation loved, respected and admired.
One of the finest managers England has produced,
this Mirror Football publication celebrates the life and times of a true legend.
Using rare archive pages and pictures from the extensive Daily Mirror collection,
his rich career is documented, from his early days as a player with England,
Fulham and West Bromwich Albion, to his many successful and varied spells in management.
Robson led unfashionable Ipswich Town to glory at home and abroad,
before taking the national team job in 1982. The finest England manager since Sir Alf Ramsey,
he twice came close to World Cup glory with England in 1986 and 1990.
He enjoyed success with clubs in Holland, Portugal and Spain,
including a memorable season at Barcelona with Jose Mourinho as his assistant
before his dream move back to his hometown club Newcastle United,
where he led the Magpies to three successive top-five finishes.
His pride in the North East is documented through his work for charity,
while his awards and achievements are also noted in this essential collection.

£4.99

ISBN 978-0-956237-34-7

9 780956 237347